The Three Reasons

Love, Music &
The San Francisco Giants

A True Story of Life After Death

Beverly Adamo

To Chiara—thank you for always being the miracle in our lives.

Contents

Introduction

Do you know why you're here on this earth? There *is* a reason
. . . sometimes there's even more than one reason. If you do
not know your reason or reasons for being here, you can
never be living life full-out. As a matter of fact, most people
are not in the process of living their lives—they're actually in
the process of dying their deaths! Living in fear and struggle,
frustration and lack is *not* living.

This book will draw you in, urge you to take a look at
your life, and inspire you to ask yourself, "What are *my* Three
Reasons for living?" You'll also learn how to take those Three
Reasons and create a life full of magic, miracles, and love, no
matter what circumstances arise, and trust me, I know first-
hand about those challenging circumstances that can arise
and attempt to pull a person under.

Through the story of my husband's unexpected death,
then his miraculous resurrection back to life, and both his
and my responses to this miracle, you'll be embarking on

your own journey of transformation. In following our journey, complete with many bleak and upsetting moments as well as blessings, you'll have us as guides, teaching and motivating you to realize your Three Reasons, then use those to completely transform both your own life and the lives of everyone around you. You'll reap the benefits of our story, perpetuating the ripple effect of miraculous, meaningful, and complete living.

Anyone who struggles with fear, frustrations, or lack of any kind will be able to use the profound wisdom and insights in this book to gain the awareness and methods for creating a life of meaning, miracles, and immediacy.

Maggie, a successful entrepreneur from California, shared, "The best thing about the book is that you simply can't put it down until you've read it cover to cover. The next best thing is that you'll be inspired to find out who *you* are, then *be* that awesome person!"

We promise that if you read this book and take the steps to bring your Three Reasons to a conscious level, you'll begin to live as you never have before. Don't wait until you die to figure out why you're alive!

While Ric proves the exception, typically, few people are able to die and bring that knowledge back to life with them so that they get a second chance at living with greater fullness, love, and meaning. Use this book to know who you are and why you're here so that you can make the biggest difference in the world *and* enjoy your life while you're making that difference.

What is it like to die and bring your reasons back with you? You're about to find out as Ric and I take you on this magic carpet ride of death . . . life . . . and . . . the magical and miraculous spaces in between!

Isn't it time you changed from dying your death to living your life?

Chapter 1

DOA – Dead on Arrival

Wednesday, January 20, 2010

In hindsight, it was probably *not* a good day to die. Ric Adamo was having one of those days when nothing seemed to be working for him. Everyone can relate to that. As his wife of almost twenty years, I was surprised when Ric called me to talk about his day. He wasn't a touchy-feely kind of person, especially when it came to talking about his feelings.

Our daughter, Chiara, was also not having a good day. Her freshman year in high school was off to a shaky start, which surprised both of us, since she had always been such a great daughter and student until then. She and I had a fight that morning before I'd even left the house to go to work, so when Ric and I were talking on the phone, he told me that he had done his best to cheer her up.

As for what wasn't working for him, well, every errand and mission he had set out to accomplish that day had failed—the persons he'd needed to see was not where they'd said they would be, there was a big rig accident on Interstate 5 that had kept him from going to a couple of places to drop off flyers, and the list went on and on.

What happened next absolutely shocked me—Ric asked me out on a date! I hadn't been very nice to him, as I recall, at the beginning of the conversation, but as we'd continued to talk, I softened and said okay, but I was still going to my yoga class as planned, and we would also ask our two favorite girls, our daughter Chiara and my mom JoAn (also known as Abba), if they wanted to come with us.

I finished my yoga class at six o'clock in the evening and headed home. Everyone was ready to go, and I decided I didn't need to change my clothes or really do anything. After all, we weren't going to stay very long at the café we were going to, and I was quite comfortable in my yoga duds.

At about 6:30 p.m., we all piled into our SUV, and Ric drove us to Main Street Jazz Café in downtown Tracy, California. There was a parking place in front of the café, and we were there to listen to the blues band playing that night. You see, just the week before, Ric and his band partner Marshall, aka Crossroads Blues Band, had played at the café, and we had met two members of the band Saturday's Blues who would be playing on this night. Ric is an awesome guitar player, and his music made me fall in love with him when we met in 1991.

We walked into the café at 6:40 p.m. as the band was playing a song. We sat at the middle table in the front part of the café and were talking about what we were going to order. We had just placed our order when the band finished playing the song and acknowledged our arrival. Mark, the band's leader, announced that the next song was dedicated to my husband, Ric Adamo, or Taildragger as he was called by his musician friends.

Ric and I were sitting directly across from each other with Chiara and my mom facing each other. As the music was playing, Ric had his arms crossed in front of him on the table, and he was smiling at me. With his eyes wide open, he slowly laid his head down on his arms, eyes still open and looking at me.

I asked, "Ric, are you alright?" As the words left my mouth, I knew he was not. I jumped up from the table and called out as I went around Chiara to reach Ric, "Call 911!"

My mom went up to the counter to repeat my request to the owner of the café to call 911. Within two seconds, I reached Ric, put my arms around him, and leaned him back upright in his chair. I looked into his eyes and urged, "Ric, stay with us," and with that, he exhaled his last breath.

It was more than a breath—not only louder, but also with more substance than just mere air. By that time, several of the people in the café had reached us and, as they took Ric to lay him down on the floor, I told them, "He's not breathing."

I turned around and asked my daughter if she could do CPR because she had just completed a babysitting class and was certified to administer CPR. As you might imagine, however, she was freaking out and admitted, "Mom, not on my own dad—I can't remember what to do!" (I know—what *was* I thinking?)

Joel, one of the young men who worked at the café, announced, "I know CPR," so he and two members of the band, Mark and Paul, began administering chest compressions. At that point, I turned to my daughter who, as I'd said, was freaking out. She had so much adrenaline in her system that she was shaking violently, vibrating at such a high rate that, for a moment, my concern was off Ric and on her. I kept telling her that everything was going to be alright and to breathe. My mom was also helping me calm my daughter.

By that time, a police officer had arrived on the scene; however, the police are prohibited from administering CPR, so all he could do was try to talk to me and get some information about Ric and what had happened.

The 911 call was made at 6:50 p.m., and the paramedics arrived around 6:58. They took over the CPR and administered defibrillation treatments—twice. Neither shock produced any results on Ric; his body simply flopped in response to the volts of electricity administered, but nothing beyond that.

One of the paramedics gathered information from me. Joel gave Chiara her smoothie. The paramedics gave me everything from Ric's pockets and the clothes they'd cut off him. Ric's body was placed onto a gurney and then loaded into the ambulance. I say his "body" because, even with the efforts to revive him, his heart still wasn't beating and he still wasn't breathing.

Chiara, my mom, and I, stunned and numb, got into our vehicle and followed the ambulance to the hospital. Even though the emergency lights for the ambulance were on, there was no siren, and we were all travelling at the speed limit.

Chiara asked me, "Mom, why are we going so slow?"

I knew the answer, but didn't want to say it.

Ric, my husband, her father—was dead.

Chapter 2

Miracle of Miracles –
44 Minutes to Life

Wednesday, January 20, 2010— *Continued*

We arrived at the hospital emergency room at approximately 7:10 p.m. I fully expected that the hospital personnel would tell me that Ric was dead . . . dead on arrival, despite all the efforts to bring him back from the full cardiac arrest that he had experienced in the café.

While we were waiting, my mom was using Ric's cell phone to try to contact Ric's son and daughter, his two brothers, and his best friend, Marshal. Nobody was answering their phones, so we left voicemails to call us as soon as they could.

A few minutes after we'd arrived at the hospital, Mark and Paul (from the band) were there to support Ric and us. I was also filling out hospital paperwork, when at about 7:45 p.m., the ambulance driver came out to have me sign the papers and to explain that I would be responsible for all charges. He was apologetic that it had to be done at a time like this, then he said something I found to be absolutely unbelievable.

The ambulance driver commented, "I think they were able to get his heart started again."

I must have looked at him in a way that either said, <u>Buddy, would you kindly speak English</u>? or perhaps, <u>You liar</u>! In either case, he backed up a step, held the papers out for me to sign, said thank you, and left.

I went back to my mom and Chiara and told them what he'd said. They both looked at me as if I were out of my mind. This just could not be.

Ten minutes later, the emergency room nurse came to get us, taking Chiara and me into the room where Ric's body was hooked up to a bunch of tubes and wires. The emergency room doctor had the strangest look on his face, as if he had just seen a ghost . . . or maybe a miracle.

The doctor explained that they were able to restart Ric's heart and that he wasn't breathing on his own. They had inserted a tube down his throat, and he was "hooked up" to a ventilator that was breathing for him. The doctor told us that they had to cut off the rest of his clothes (as if I might actually care about *that*), and now they were going to move him to the intensive care unit (ICU).

I think I replied, "Okay," or something like that. Actually, perhaps surprisingly, I felt extremely calm. Much more calm than the emergency room doctor, in any case. Looking back, I can see that from the moment Ric's head started dropping down to the table at the café, even though I'd been taking action from that moment on, my emotions had been in neutral. There was simply too much going on for me to be on any emotional roller coaster. I had stepped off the ride and was doing what was needed and observing all the rest.

The doctor told us that it was hard to say if Ric would last long. The next four hours would tell us more. I could tell that the doctor didn't want us to get our hopes up that Ric would recover.

The doctor also explained that this never happened, someone coming back after being without a heartbeat and breath for such an extended period. "People don't come back from a full cardiac arrest," he reported. "It's not as it's portrayed on television. Most people do *not* come back."

Yet, there was Ric with a heartbeat, and he was breathing (or I should say, the machine was breathing for him).

The doctor repeated, "People don't come back," and he wandered, a bit dazed, from the room.

The emergency room nurse told us, "We're going to move him now. You can come up with us, but then you'll have to stay in the waiting room until we get him settled."

13

As the nurse went to prepare for the transport, he suggested, "Talk to him. Hearing is the last sense to go. He can hear you."

As you'll see, that became my mantra over the next 24 hours.

I went up the elevator with Ric while Chiara informed her grandmother of what was happening. Once I reached the ICU, I stayed in the waiting room, then Chiara and my mom joined me. We still hadn't reached anyone by phone; however, by that time, the two band members who had performed CPR met us in the ICU waiting room.

Once Ric was settled into his room, the nurse told me I could see him. I walked through the locked doors, pulled up a chair next to his bed, and began talking to him. I spoke about how much I loved him, told him that I wasn't sure what to do, and asked if he could tell me or show me what to do. I spoke about Chiara and told him, if he could, to please let her know how much he loved her and that no matter what, she would be alright, that everything would be alright.

I remember thinking, how in the world can everything 'be alright' when her dad just died, yet that was what I asked for.

It was strange to see Ric so still. His hands were warm as I held them. Shortly thereafter, I went back out to the waiting room and asked Chiara and Mom to go home. Though Chiara wasn't going to school the next day, they both needed to get some rest if they could. They went in to see Ric before they left, and I told them, "Talk to him—he can hear you."

That first night, as I sat alone by Ric's side, I thought of our life together—when and how we'd met, the years of our marriage, and the birth of Chiara. It was as though I were experiencing my own version of a life review. My life with Ric.

It was strange to feel the warmth of his hand and see the body that lay there in that bed, and at the same time know that his essence, his soul, that which made the body that lay there in that bed, the person we knew and loved, was somewhere else. Where *was* Ric?

Even though I knew and believed that he could hear and see us, he wasn't there in his body. His body was so still even with all the activity that was around us through the night—doctors, a neurologist, a lung doctor, a respiratory therapist, nurses. All of the hospital staff who attended Ric spoke to him in loud voices, addressing him directly and telling him exactly what they were going to do, taking blood, administering drugs, adjusting this or that.

I didn't sleep at all that night.

Thursday, January 21, 2010

The next morning, I left the ICU to go to the bathroom, and upon my return the first person I saw entering the ICU waiting room was Ric's son, Kit. The two of them had been estranged for many years, yet Kit was the first one through the doors. I felt such a love for Kit at that moment; I gave him a big hug and walked him into the room where his dad was lying and told him, "Talk to him. He can hear you."

If you've ever had a friend or loved one in the intensive care unit in the hospital, you know that visitors are strictly regulated, and when visitors are allowed, it's usually one person at a time. All during that day, more people arrived: Ric's best friend and band mate Marshal and his wife, Amy; Ric's brother Len and his wife, Peggy; Ric's daughter Carrie and her husband, Mike; and Ric's granddaughter, Rachel.

It was uplifting to see all the people who cared about us and made the trip to the hospital, given only a few hours' notice. Some had travelled great distances. Chiara was there, of course, along with my mom. As each person came to that waiting room, they got their turn alone with Ric, talking to him because he could hear them.

All day long, a recurring thought I had was that Ric had come back in this comatose state, his body still alive, but his spirit nowhere to be found, for people to say goodbye. I thought, what a gift to his family, to die so quickly and painlessly, yet come back (in a manner of speaking) so that everyone can say goodbye and have a chance to speak their piece, even if Ric isn't physically able to answer.

That night when the neurologist came by, I asked her whether there was any brain activity. That was my biggest concern. Ric hated being hooked up to things in the hospital and had a DNR (do not resuscitate) order on file (of course, that's not something I thought about when I'd rounded the table and yelled, "Call 911!").

The neurologist responded that there was no bleeding in his brain (CATSCAN showed that), which was good news. Still, when she came to describing Ric's brain activity, she seemed to be searching for just the right word. Finally, after long consideration, she divulged, "Sluggish . . . his brain activity is sluggish."

I wanted to tell her to go back into that brain of hers and come up with a different word. "Sluggish" wasn't what I wanted to hear; it didn't sound very promising to me, which is why it was the right word—Ric's condition wasn't promising.

When I asked if she thought Ric would be able to breathe on his own, she replied, "Hard to say." I think it was hard to say because the answer was no.

Again, I spent Thursday night with Ric, alone, truly alone because the essence and soul that was Ric was not there. Chiara and my mom went back home because Chiara needed to go to school the next day, at least to get her homework assignments and have her school assignments for the weekend. Looking back, I know that it was silly of me to expect that Chiara would have *any* kind of focus for school. Nevertheless, it was just what came to us to do, and, at that point, I was following a Divine guidance that was beyond my ability to think.

It was a long night for me because Ric had fluid and junk (I know there's a better medical term for it, but, to me, it was "junk") forming in his lungs. The respiratory therapist (RT) would come in to clear his lungs manually every so often. It was a horrible experience to hear the sounds and see the junk that would come out of the tube forced down his throat, but the reward was that the machine was better able to do its job of breathing for Ric.

The RT informed me that this process was akin to coughing and that Ric was sometimes coughing on his own, his body helping to rid itself of the junk. God, it was awful to hear and watch, but I didn't leave, couldn't leave. Sometimes, when I was alone with him and it seemed as though he were going to die trying to breathe through the junk, I would step out of the room and quietly ask if someone could help him.

The ICU personnel were responsive and kind, although sometimes it seemed like an eternity before they responded to my request for help as I watched Ric's body struggle to breathe through the junk. I remember thinking that it was fortunate that Ric himself was definitely not in his body.

In addition to talking with Ric almost nonstop, I also believe in the healing power of touch, so I would work my way up and down his still body with my hands, touching his forehead and arms, resting my hands gently on his chest. The hospital staff had wrapped Ric's legs in devices that were designed to keep the blood in his legs circulating even though he couldn't move. I knew what they were from my own experiences after surgery, yet Ric's feet were so cold, it was as though his heart was working, but wasn't quite strong enough to circulate the blood all the way down the length of his legs to his feet and toes.

The experience of holding his hand, which was as warm as ever, was so surreal, knowing that I was touching his hand, but that Ric wasn't there. Doctors and nurses would also take his hand and say, "Squeeze my hand." Repeatedly, anyone who came in would do this in an effort to see some kind of response from him, but there was none.

Ric, his essence, was still gone.

Chapter 3

A Hero's Journey –
Ric's Second Birth-day

Friday, January 22, 2010

The doctors and I could see that there was more going on with Ric's body. His essence, his soul, was not yet back, but his body seemed to have an innate somatic intelligence that said, <u>Hey, I need to be moving and up and around</u>. His eyes were starting to open. He was thrashing about more and more. He even seemed to be attempting to remove the breathing tube from his throat.

After a conference with the doctors, including the neurologist, I asked them to go ahead and take him off the medication that was keeping him in a medically induced coma so he could "wake up" as much as was possible. I knew that doing this might very well result in Ric's true and final death; however, I kept thinking about the fact that he hated being hooked up to anything in the hospital.

Ric had had a knee replacement a few years prior, and he'd told me then that if he was ever in the hospital and unable to make the choice on his own, that he wanted to be "unhooked" and have any machines "turned off." That was when we both chose to put DNR (do not resuscitate) orders on file.

After a few hours of watching Ric's body "wake up," I was in a place of faith and peace when I told the doctors that we needed to remove the breathing tube to see if Ric could breathe on his own. I explained to the doctors that he would never want to be connected to all the tubes and wires that were currently keeping him "alive." I was told that I would be able to be in the room with Ric during this procedure, and soon the breathing tube was out and an oxygen mask placed over his face.

I vividly and will forever remember what happened next. Ric's efforts to breathe on his own were absolutely heroic. They were monumental, elemental, and heartbreaking. The doctor quickly ushered me out of the room, asserting, "We have to reintubate him. He can not continue trying to breathe like this on his own. Either his heart or his lungs or both will give out, and he's not taking in enough oxygen to sustain his life."

Ric's brother Len had joined me outside of the room and was standing beside me as the doctor advised me on what needed to be done. There was a moment of intense confusion in my mind and body, followed immediately by an infinite calm. There was no hesitation as I decided, "No, we will not do that. This is between Ric and his Maker."

To their credit, neither Len nor the doctor argued the point. The doctor told me he would call the counselor from the hospital to meet with me regarding actions we needed to take after Ric passed away. The hospital staff would prepare the room for family to be with Ric, and they would make Ric as comfortable as possible (meaning removing most of the tubes, etc.).

It's ironic how doctors consider their efforts to extend someone's life with all their latest drugs, techniques, and machinery as "heroic." There's nothing heroic about turning a human being into a vegetable.

I went out to the waiting room and told everyone of the decision and that they should call anyone else who might want to be there to say goodbye. I asked Len and my mom to go to the school, pick up Chiara, and bring her to the hospital.

The hospital counselor found me and led me to his office. He gave me literature on cremation, burial, funeral homes, etc. The only thing I really heard and remembered was what he said as we ended our conversation. He thanked me, sharing that of all the family members he had talked with over the years, the conversation we'd just had was filled with such grace and dignity with respect to Ric that he was deeply moved. (I wish I could remember what I'd said to elicit this from him.)

When Len, my mom, and Chiara arrived, all I could do for a while was hug my daughter. Len and his wife, Peggy, and the hospital chaplain joined my mom, Chiara, and me as we went back into Ric's room. I'll always remember the courage and determination Chiara showed as she entered this room where her beloved father lay dying. Her actions and love were as heroic as her father's.

The ICU room had an air of peace and love, with only one exception; the sounds of Ric literally reaching out and grasping great pockets of life-giving oxygen to bring back into his lungs, then expelling the carbon dioxide in a gust of equally intense effort. Even if I used the word "heroic" a million times to describe his efforts to keep his body alive, the description would still be understated.

We all spoke with Ric, telling him it was okay to do whatever he needed to do, that we would be alright and that we loved him. We talked with him about times we remembered and enjoyed. We sang to him. We laughed. We cried. We literally surrounded him and ourselves with love and permission to be in that moment, every moment, with him in what we all thought at the time was his process of dying (for the final time).

As the hours passed, though, the effort it took for Ric to breathe lessened, and the oxygen level in his blood increased to an acceptable level. Once more, evidently, it wasn't Ric's time to die. Hospital staff hooked his body back up to the monitoring devices and put the IV back that was providing him with sustenance.

One by one, we all left the room to go about the business of taking care of our own bodily functions and needs. I stayed until I was the only one with Ric once again. It occurred to me that I would continue to be in that room, with the exception of bathroom breaks, quick meetings with family and friends, and consults with doctors and the counselor. My mom and friends made sure I had something to eat at regular intervals but, for the most part, I was in that room with my husband or, I should say, my husband's physical body.

By that evening, there had been more tests, and any number of doctors and nurses coming by, asking Ric to squeeze their hand. Ric's body continued to "wake up," and his eyes were mostly open and would wander to different points in the room, although not as a response to any stimulus. If someone would talk to him, he was just as likely to be "looking" at a point in the room that was opposite to the person who was speaking his name. It was quite fascinating to have the man I had been married to for almost twenty years "looking" at me and absolutely knowing that he wasn't there and that no one was "seeing" me.

A point of interest that I noticed from the moment Ric arrived in the ICU room was that all of his nurses, technicians, aids, and doctors, were beautiful people! Especially, the women were gorgeous without exception, and I thought with a smile how perfectly "Ric" this was, surrounded by gorgeous women.

His respiratory therapist was no exception. She was beautiful and had such an amazing smile. She had been in many times over the course of the previous 48 hours and had been the one who'd told me about Ric's "coughing" and clearing his lungs. That night, she was in the room at the machine providing oxygen to Ric through his mask. She and the machine were on the left side of Ric's bed, I was at the foot of the bed, and Chiara was on his right side.

I already mentioned that staff all spoke to Ric in a loud voice when they were informing him about exactly what they were doing. I never bothered with the loud voice. I believed that wherever Ric was, he could likely hear me just fine, even if I were whispering or talking to him in my thoughts.

The hospital bed was adjusted so that Ric was in a semi-reclined position, and as I mentioned, Ric had his eyes open. The respiratory therapist was about to make some adjustment to the oxygen machine when she said quite loudly, "RIC—" but before she could say anything else, Ric turned his head to her and smiled his big smile.

I knew—RIC WAS BACK!

Chapter 4

A Magic Carpet Ride – Part 1

Friday, January 22, 2010—*Continued*

As you can imagine, everyone was amazed as word spread that Ric's spirit had returned to his body! In more medical terms, Ric had awakened from his coma.

The doctor was called to the room, and he approached the side of Ric's bed and took Ric's hand. This time, when the doctor said, "Squeeze my hand," Ric did so! The doctor looked at him and inquired, "Do you know your last name?"

Ric replied, "Adamo."

The doctor pointed to me where I stood at the other side of the hospital bed and asked, "Do you know who that is?"

Ric looked at me and answered, "My wife."

The doctor pointed to our daughter at the foot of Ric's bed and asked, "Do you know who that is?"

Without hesitation, Ric answered, "Chiara."

A couple of notes of interest. First, because there had been a tube down his throat for 36 hours or so, when Ric spoke, his voice had a whispery, gruff quality. If you saw the movie *The Godfather* with Marlon Brando and remember the quality of Brando's voice, Ric sounded just like him. Second, my husband is a smart man, and as we came to find out, had experienced a good deal of interesting happenings with his brain and how it was then working after his death experience (more about that later).

When the doctor asked him who I was, although there was no hesitation in his answer, he didn't say my name; he said I was "his wife." That still makes me laugh because Ric had been married three times before we were married! As for his daughter Chiara, well, there was neither a hesitation nor an equivocating response. Ric knew his daughter even through the veil of death!

Ric returned to his body during the evening hours of that Friday, and there weren't a lot of people left at the hospital. I eventually sent my mom and Chiara home for the night to get some rest and to call everyone with the latest update. Soon, I was alone with my husband, and he was talking. The next ten hours or so turned into an interesting odyssey.

Ric spoke to me of many things, including asking me to marry him (he didn't propose prior to our marriage, but that's another story, so his proposal on that special night of his second birth-day made me cry; it so touched my heart).

He spoke of music, baseball, and his father, who had passed away more than five years before. There was such a quality of unconditional love surrounding Ric and his words. We didn't talk about what had happened and why he was in the hospital. It's funny now that I think about it, but it just wasn't the topic of our conversations.

Still in the ICU, the hospital staff would come in and out at regular intervals, checking on this and that, or taking blood or samples for testing. For the most part though, consensus was that Ric's condition was still quite grave and that he wouldn't likely last the night.

During those dark hours, there were times when Ric was still and both of us would nap, he in the bed and me in the chair, leaning over the bed and holding his hand. This was probably the best place for me to be because, without warning, Ric would try to get out of the bed, so I would startle awake and soothe him and help him back into the bed.

As the night went on, he would alternate between his quiet, soothing state of unconditional love and a state of frenetic activity during which he would say over and over again, "I don't know if I can do this . . . I don't know if I can stay."

During the time that he was speaking to me, there were only two points that I knew he was speaking to his wife, but *not* to me. Again, I was his fourth marriage! When I would ask him who he thought I was, he would pause, give one of his ex-wives' names, then look at me again, and say, "No, you're Bev." I didn't take it personally. After all, the man had died and come back through who knows what to be here in this room with me!

Saturday, January 23, 2010

By morning, though, he seemed to be more stable, and as people arrived again at the hospital, he started to receive visitors. To a person, he remembered everyone who came to see him, and some of them he hadn't seen in years. Interestingly, he had no short-term memory. That meant that I would bring people into the room, and he would greet them enthusiastically by name and talk to them coherently (he still didn't have his fine motor functions intact, but his speech was great).

If people would leave for a bit, then return, Ric would again greet them enthusiastically, as though it had been years since he had last seen them, even though it might have been only a few minutes. Chiara, my mom, and I seemed to be the exception to that rule. The fact that we were coming and going on a regular basis seemed to stay in his short-term memory, but it was as if he didn't have room for anyone else in that space in his brain.

The experience was more disconcerting to everyone else who was visiting. They were quite amazed that he seemed so cognizant of who they were and what was going on but didn't remember they had just been in to see him.

Then there was his dad. Ric kept asking if we had let his dad know what had happened. I told him that his dad knew what happened. He had no memory that his dad was dead. Ric didn't remember anything of the estrangement with his son either, and that was a blessing for both of them.

At one point, the doctor asked him if he knew what year it was, and Ric responded, "Two thousand two." Who's the president? "George W. Bush." Ric didn't seem too bothered by the fact that it was actually 2010 when he would be reminded of that; however, he was highly pissed off that Obama was president (no offense to President Obama or any of his supporters—Ric has always been a staunch Republican, and that's definitely one of the things that did *not* change even through his death experience).

During the day on Saturday, January 23, between visitors, Ric, of course, had a great many specialists who examined him. There were two things that they seemed particularly interested in. The first was his ejection fraction, which is expressed in a percentage and speaks to how well the heart pumps with each beat. Evidently, it was at a level that shouldn't have sustained Ric's being alive.

The doctors would tell me these things, then look at me as though I should be able to respond as to how this man was evidently performing miracle after miracle. What could I say? I was just along for the ride, this magic carpet ride.

Of course, when I looked into this ejection fraction later and learned that a normal rate is 55 percent to 75 percent and that Ric's rate at the time during the first few days after his death was at less than 10 percent, I could see why the doctors weren't understanding why Ric didn't die again.

The second phenomenon that so interested the medical team was Ric's swallowing reflex. Being intubated can result in major issues with swallowing. I know this based on a later experience with my aunt, who was intubated for weeks and had major, long-term therapy to get back her ability to swallow, etc. (I suggest you look this up if you want to understand all the issues that can happen.)

The specialist was again surprised that Ric didn't seem to have any of those issues with swallowing or with his speech as a result of the intubation. I believe that making the decision to remove the tube so early in Ric's "coma period" was a blessing now that he was, at least for the moment, back in the land of the living.

That day, Ric began to eat soft but "real" food, and I was happy to help "feed" him. As I mentioned before, while Ric's speech was almost immediately back to normal, his ability to use his arms and the dexterity of his hands were somewhat absent. *That* was what scared me. You see, Ric had played the guitar since he was a young teenager, and the thought of what would happen to him if he could no longer do that, well—it was something that I didn't want to contemplate, so I didn't.

Instead, I started to notice that in some ways, Ric seemed to be "tripping." Mind you, I had made the request that Ric, under no circumstances, be given the morphine that he had been prescribed for arthritic pain prior to his death experience. Morphine was a drug that Ric reacted badly to because it brought out a rageful and totally mean aspect of his personality. The drugs that were being administered were limited to what he had been taking for his heart health, yet he was undeniably "tripping."

At one point, Ric was talking to me and a friend who was in the room when he suddenly noticed the pulse/oxygen monitor clamped onto his index finger. Granted, it did have an eerie, psychedelic red glow to it that seemed to render the tip of his finger transparent and bright red. His arm and hand movements were clumsy, which was why I helped him eat those meals that were brought to him.

When Ric noticed this finger, all of his attention immediately went to that appendage. He moved it slowly and in a figure eight, apparently trying to stop the motion of his arm, but being unsuccessful in doing so. As he watched the glow that seemed to have a mind of its own, he said in a slow and drugged voice, "W-o-o-o-w-w-w-w-w . . . Th-a-a-a-a-a-t's c-o-o-o-o-o-o-o-l!"

There were many experiences that we had over the months of Ric's recovery to which I managed to assign my own interpretation, and this was one of them. What I deduced happened was that some of the LSD that he had taken in his teen years and in his twenties had managed to be stored in cells in his body, so with the "hard reboot" that had happened with his death experience, some of those drugs were released into his system. There just wasn't anything that he was given at the time that would have resulted in some of his responses. It was quite amusing!

I, in return, was quite amusing to Ric as well. Prior to his death, Ric had suffered from severe arthritis in various parts of his body, including his hands. The severe arthritis was one of the reasons Ric had been prescribed the morphine. None of the other pain drugs were working anymore. While he could still play guitar, he was unable to make a fist with either of his hands, and he couldn't bend his fingers and curl them together into his palms.

At one point during that Saturday, as I was sitting by his bedside, he simply made a fist, then opened his hand. I grabbed his wrist and practically yelled at him, "Do that *again*!"

Ric was a little startled, but when he saw what I meant, as I made a fist and opened my own hand, he mimicked the motion. I laughed with delight, which brought a smile to his face, so he opened his fist, then made another one! Another laugh of delight! Now with both hands!

Fortunately for us, there wasn't anyone else in the room, or they might have thought we were both candidates for the psychiatric ward.

It was amazing that what he couldn't do prior to his death, he now had no trouble doing. When he asked why I was so amazed, I mentioned that he had been taking morphine for the pain he was in, and he emphatically stated, "I do *not* take morphine!" Well, to be fair, in 2002, he didn't use morphine. Taking morphine only happened a year or so before he died.

The mind is so powerful, sometimes even more powerful than the body. Later I came to understand that there were a number of "pathways" in Ric's brain that had either been erased, or the connection to Ric's consciousness had been severed. Whatever actually happened, the results were intriguing and interesting.

Now for some information regarding the environment: hospitals are not a place to heal. I'm making an observation here, not passing judgment. There are no usual day or night light cues for the body and mind, and even if Ric hadn't actually died, then come back from that death journey, it's likely that he may have experienced some sensory hallucinations and memory loss.

There's something particularly challenging about nighttime in hospitals. Ask anyone who works that shift. During the day, the nurses usually had the blinds open, so that at least there was a semblance of daytime; however, with everything that was going on, this wasn't always the best for Ric. This wasn't the first time Ric had been hospitalized, although it was definitely the most time he'd spent in the ICU, and this experience was far more critical than any other time.

I became aware that Ric was experiencing a phenomenon called "sundowning," which refers to a state of confusion that happens at the end of the day and into the night. If you talk to health care professionals, in and outside of hospitals, they're aware of this phenomenon, and it was something that the staff talked to me about.

Sundowning can cause a variety of behaviors in a person, such as confusion, anxiety, aggression, or ignoring directions. Some of the factors that I learned of that can aggravate late-day confusion include fatigue, low lighting, increased shadows, and disruption of the body's "internal clock," all of which can lead to a person experiencing difficulty separating reality from dreams.

Other environmental factors can cause it, too, like being thrust into unfamiliar hospitals with bright fluorescent lights, having sticky heart monitors on your chest, and hearing alarm bells going off at all hours of the night.

Thankfully, not every hospital patient "sundowns;" however, when one does, it can be emotionally traumatizing for everyone. That's one of the reasons I always made sure Chiara and my mom went home at night, and I was the only family member spending the night with Ric.

On this particular night, we moved into the night from hell . . . and (sigh of relief) the morning of heaven.

I mentioned how Ric could recognize people he knew, but if they left the room and shortly returned, it was as if he were seeing them for the first time in a long time, instead of only minutes later. That continued to happen. There was another phenomenon that also started to occur. I call it "looping." What would happen is this:

Ric: I gotta pee!

Nurse, Bev, or both: Go ahead, you have a catheter.

Ric: No, I don't, and I gotta pee! It's going to get all over the bed.

Nurse, Bev, or both: No. You have a catheter. Go ahead and pee.

Ric: I don't have a catheter, and I gotta go.

Nurse, Bev, or both: Here, let us show you. See the tube? [*Showing Ric the apparatus*]

Ric: O-h-h-h-h-h-h-h-h-h-h. Okay. That's so great! Thank you!

[*Moments of silence*]

***Ric*:** I gotta pee!

Here we go again.

This would continue for minutes sometimes and for hours other times. Every time there was a shift change, the "I gotta pee" loop would kick in. There were times when the nurses just couldn't hold back the laughter, and I would encourage them not to hold it back. After all, it was hysterical, and the best thing about it was that if we laughed, Ric would usually join us, so it was a good thing for all.

That night, there was also the hellish part. Even though I had convinced the staff not to give Ric any morphine, it wasn't on his list of medications, and there shouldn't have been any medication that would stimulate him into anger or rage, he would get into a place where he was simply wild.

He had always been a strong man, and with the changes that had happened and were happening in his brain, God only knows the chemicals his own body was releasing into his system. At times, Ric was screaming, thrashing, and trying to get out of bed. It literally took four nurses and me to keep him in the bed.; then the proverbial shit hit the fan. Literally.

During one of the major WWF (World Wrestling Federation) events when we were trying to keep Ric in the bed and Ric was doing his best to climb out of it, Ric had a bowel movement. Now why would I want to write about that? As you can imagine, it was one of those truly human moments (or series of moments) when we didn't know whether to laugh or cry, and all of us, including Ric, were doing it all.

Once everyone and the room were cleaned up again, one of the nurses looked at me and insisted, "Mrs. Adamo! You have to get some rest. If you won't go home, then curl up in the reclining chair over there and let us care for your husband for a few hours."

That was what I did. There were moments when I would be brought out of my exhausted sleep by the yelling and a lot of movement in the room, but I was so tired that I couldn't manage to bring myself back to full consciousness, and I slept.

Sunday, January 24, 2010

When I awoke, it was to a quiet that I wasn't sure at first was real. Instead of the bright lights that were usually on in the room, the curtains were closed, and the lights were dimmed. I could see that Ric was resting with eyes closed (not sure if he was actually sleeping), and all seemed to be well.

I noticed a couple of details as my eyes adjusted to being awake. Ric was literally tied to the bed by his ankles and wrists, and there was a young woman quietly sitting in a chair on the opposite side of Ric's bed.

At first, I wasn't sure that she was real, but then she quietly said, "Good morning," so I knew that she was actually there. She went to get a nurse, and the nurse explained that they finally had to secure Ric to the bed for his own good. He had ripped out so many of the IVs from his veins that he was actually injuring himself, not to mention depriving his body of the needed fluids.

As Ric came back into consciousness, he seemed much calmer and wanted to know why his hands were tied down. I explained it was to make sure the IVs stayed in place since his body seemed to be a bit restless at times (a gross understatement, but what the heck).

I was still exhausted, and I could tell Ric was as well. I made a decision that there would be no visitors that day and called my mom to ask her to spread the word. I remember telling my mom that we had a *bad* night and that visitors that morning were simply out of the question.

In addition, the hospital staff had also advised me that they felt Ric was stable enough to be moved to a facility about twenty miles away, where our insurance would be able to cover completely the costs of his care and where the doctors would then be able to make some decisions about what was next.

The doctors felt that if Ric continued to improve, he would likely need to have a stent placed in an artery to clear a blockage, and he would need a defibrillator installed in his chest to ensure that if there were another cardiac arrest, the defibrillator would restart his heart immediately (or attempt to).

That morning, with a little restless sleep to help me along, I saw the young lady—I'm not sure if they still call them "candy stripers" anymore; she did have that red-and-white striped smock over her clothes—and she seemed to be a quiet angel watching over us. Ric, however, saw her in an entirely different perspective as I soon learned when he motioned for me to come closer, so he could whisper to me without her hearing him, "Do you see that on the chair?"

I replied, "You mean the young lady there?"

He seemed both relieved and still quite anxious as he confided, "Yes, so she's real? I thought I was imagining her."

I confirmed, "Yes, she's real."

With his next words, I discovered the source of his anxiety. Ric revealed, "She's the devil here to take me to hell."

Alrighty then . . .

Throughout our many conversations over the previous few days, I'd told him the truth sometimes; other times, I'd told him whatever it felt like he wanted to hear or I'd said nothing. This was one of the times when I said nothing. I simply waited to hear what else Ric thought I should know about this angelic devil who had come back into the room and was silently watching over us.

Ric proceeded to tell me that there had been a number of things he had done during his life that he should go to hell for. While there were things he had done that I could remember in the time I knew him that pissed me off, I didn't know of any, at least from that period of his life, which would have sentenced him to purgatory, let alone hell.

Ric was an altar boy, raised in a Catholic family, so what did I know? At the very least, in my exhausted mind at the time, I wondered if there was any way that I could help put him at ease, so here's how it went.

"Ric, you know how spiritually 'connected' I am, right?" I'm exceptionally intuitive and a woman of complete faith. We often had discussions during which Ric would be worried about something, and I would assure him that everything was going to work out perfectly. He would later ask me how I could have possibly known that something so screwed up could "work out perfectly." I would always respond to him with these same words—because I have faith!

My uncanny ability to understand what was going on in our lives at any given moment and know where we were likely to end up was not only something that scared Ric but also something he loved about me. In asking that question, unless he had lost all of his memories of our life together, I could anticipate that he would respond in the affirmative, which he did.

"Ric, I can absolutely tell you that this young lady is definitely not a messenger from the devil. She has nothing but purity and grace in her heart when it comes to you."

horse revolution —

horses saddled
up humans and
rode into the sunset

2

Ric looked at me, then at the young lady, then back at me. "You're sure?"

I answered with a smile, "Yes, I am."

At that, Ric seemed to relax, at least a bit, and smiled at me, then for the first time, at the young lady. I silently breathed a sigh of relief. Plus, Ric was still tied to the bed, so the possibility that he would be able to get up and launch himself out of the bed at anyone was fairly remote.

Okay—for now.

Chapter 5

Magic Carpet Ride – Part 2

Sunday, January 24, 2010— *Continued*

Ric and I were able to "rest" for an hour or so until hospital staff called me out to the nurses' station. They had been able to determine that Ric could be transported via ambulance to the hospital where the doctors would devise what was next.

After I'd spent some time at the nurses' station doing the necessary paperwork, it was time for a much needed bio break. It was when I walked out of the hallway and down to the restroom that I realized that I was still in my "yoga duds" from Wednesday night! Oh, well, nobody was complaining about how I smelled (yet), and the clothes were extremely comfortable, thank goodness!

By the time I returned to the nurses' station, I could see that the ambulance drivers were there, taking care of their paperwork. Before I went in to talk to Ric, I stopped and introduced myself to the drivers. One of them lowered his voice and inquired, "Mrs. Adamo, why is he tied to the bed?" Now how do I answer that? Ric is a big, Italian man, who even after dying and returning, at six feet three inches tall and 250 pounds of solid muscle, looked quite formidable.

Smiling, I assured them that it was for Ric's protection, to keep him from ripping out the tubes, rather than for the protection of those around him. Since I had been able to keep the morphine out of his system, my explanation was still mainly true. Aggression toward anyone else wasn't likely when he wasn't on the morphine.

Of course, in the past, raising his voice wasn't reserved for morphine since Ric maintained that in a good Italian household, no conversation was held at less than a yelling decibel. No matter how many times I reminded him I was only Italian by marriage, he would tell me, "Same thing applies."

In any case, obviously Ric was still tied to the bed when the ambulance folks arrived and had been into Ric's room to introduce themselves. When I went in to see Ric, again, he motioned me to come closer, so he could whisper, "This is probably the last time you'll see me alive."

WTF! My response, "Okay, Ric, why is that?"

"Well, the boys from the neighborhood. They're here to take me back 'cause we gotta face the music."

Pretty cliché if you ask me, but I could see that Ric was completely serious. I asked what he meant, and he explained that he was going for a ride with these boys back to the neighborhood and that they had to take care of some business. According to Ric, these boys worked with him at the piano store he'd worked in for many years in Los Angeles. Ric then proceeded to describe to me the "old neighborhood" and how there would be people behind every window who would be "gunning for them."

Over the course of our marriage, Ric had told me some pretty hair-raising stories. At no time did he hurt nor kill anyone, and I'm trusting that for the crimes he probably did commit in those crazy sex-drugs-and-rock-n-roll days, the statutes had run out many decades ago!

There was a slight possibility that he may have exaggerated those stories just for the shock effect it always had on Miss Goody-Two-Shoes (that would be me, of course). As the hospital and ambulance staff prepared Ric for his journey, I could understand why he thought this would be the last time I might see him! Yikes!

When Ric was transported via ambulance to the medical facility twenty miles away, I didn't accompany him. Instead, I took the opportunity to go home and take a shower for the first time since his event (why I didn't think I could leave his side until then, I'm not sure. It just hadn't seemed like what I should do).

After the quick shower, it was time to drive to the hospital where Ric was being transported. Just like Ric, this was the first time I was out of the hospital since we'd arrived on January 20. It was also the first time that Ric was really "alone" with people since he'd died.

While I can imagine the conversation Ric had with the guys in the ambulance, evidently it was much more wild than even my imagination was capable of. When I arrived at the hospital, I ran into "the boys" as they were leaving, and they asked me a question that, as it turned out, I was going to be hearing a lot of going forward: "Is your husband always like this?"

My internal response, <u>well . . . let me think . . . probably not! The man died just days ago. Just what are you health care professionals really asking?</u>

Externally, I just smiled, thanked "the boys" for Ric's safe delivery to this destination, and proceeded to the ICU.

I had to wait for a bit for the nurses to get Ric settled in the ICU of the hospital. Until that time, I had managed to circumvent anyone's attempt to give him morphine although as I mentioned, it was in his medical record and showed that it was clearly prescribed to him prior to his death.

When I arrived at the unit, I could tell that he was "different." I asked the nurse whether he had been given any drugs. They told me what they had given him and, sure enough, it included morphine! I was angry, but mostly at myself for not having been there to tell them otherwise.

Even before his heart event, the morphine prescribed to Ric for pain gave him what I called a mean edge. He was always rather volatile, and I attributed that to his Italian heritage and the fact that, from what I could tell, he had a lifetime of never having learned much self-control. In any case, I could tell that in his current state, without some of the filters that existed prior to the hard reboot of his brain, the morphine unleashed Ric's darkest parts.

I spent a couple of hours with him, but at a certain point, I was simply too exhausted to continue to deal with the effects of the drug and his treatment of me. Even though I had only been there for a couple of hours, I advised the nurse that I was leaving for the night and literally ran out to my car.

Once inside the car, I slammed and locked the door and proceeded to scream at the top of my lungs at God, "TAKE HIM BACK! TAKE HIM BACK! TAKE HIM BACK!" That probably lasted for three minutes or so, then I started laughing hysterically! Good thing the parking lot was deserted!

When I arrived home, I was still giggling a bit and, of course, my daughter came tiptoeing out of her room and snuggled next to me as I vacillated between tears and laughter. "Mom, is dad okay?" I managed to tell her that yes, he was, then I was telling her about the morphine fiasco, including my demanding God to "TAKE HIM BACK!" and we were both covering our mouths and trying to stifle our hysterics, so we wouldn't wake my mom. Soon, though, we both were sound asleep.

Monday, January 25, 2010

At six o'clock the next morning, the ICU nurse called me, and the first question she asked was (you guessed it) "Is your husband always this way?" They experienced first-hand the full effects of "Ric on morphine" even though they had taken the prescription off his list of meds when I told them to before I ran out of there the night before. If Ric hadn't been so deathly ill, I have a feeling that those nurses would have cheerfully given him the boot, and I wouldn't have blamed them one bit!

I made it to the hospital and, thanks to a little rest and the emotional release that came with the screaming and laughing, I was again in a mental, emotional, and spiritual willingness to be with Ric during that day. Chiara visited after school (yes, she was back in school), and Ric's youngest brother, Michael, arrived that evening to see him.

Ric, by that time, had burned most of the morphine out of his system and was a bit saner. Or maybe I was now a bit saner, so I could be patient with Ric again, no matter what.

That evening, Ric told Michael and me some of the things he was "remembering" from his journey to the great beyond and back. He also talked about traveling the world, playing rock-and-roll music, and playing baseball with "the guys" (albeit different "guys" than "the boys" who'd transported him to this hospital). During this time, Ric told us the interesting story about his doctor.

Ric's primary physician had been caring for Ric since before he was diagnosed with congestive heart failure four years previously in December 2006. I remember the day, December 15, 2006, to be exact, because Ric had said he wasn't feeling too good.

I took one look at my husband and announced, "We're going to see the doctor now."

Once we were at the office, the doctor took one listen to Ric's heart and hooked him up for an EKG. Moments after looking at those results, the doctor called an ambulance, and Ric was transported to the hospital to begin treatment for congestive heart failure.

By the grace of God, Ric didn't die in December 2006, but the doctor said it was close. We weren't sure he would be home that Christmas or home at all. During his stay of nine days, Ric "lost" 27 pounds of water weight, and so began Ric's journey of losing a total of one hundred pounds over the course of the next year.

Because of the congestive heart failure, Ric's doctor and a heart nurse were in contact with him consistently from 2006 through 2010, so it didn't surprise me too much when Ric started "remembering" his doctor.

Back to what Ric was telling us about his "journey to and beyond death." First, he told us that he'd found himself fishing on the banks of his favorite stream in the mountains and noticed his dad was there, too. His dad had asked him, "What the fuck are you doing here?" (There's something about the F-word that just naturally rolls off the Italian tongue, even in death, as Ric's dad died in 2003).

Ric responded, "Hey, I'm fishing!" His dad told him that he couldn't stay, and with that, Ric said that he then started "dreaming."

Ric said that in his "dream," he found himself out on the streets, not knowing who he was or where he was. He had an overcoat on though, and in the pocket of the coat was a business card. It had the name of his doctor on it with the doctor's address. He was able to get to his doctor's office, and when he met with the doc, Ric's first question was "Doctor, do you know who I am?"

The doctor replied, "Of course, I know who you are. You're Ric Adamo, and you've been my patient for many years." At that point, Ric explained that he hadn't known his own name or anything about himself. He told the doctor that he had a great pain in the center of his forehead, actually more in the center of his brain.

The doctor listened with great interest and patience, and when Ric was done describing what he was feeling, the doctor determined, "I know exactly what's wrong. You have a brain worm, and we need to get it out of your head."

Ric admitted that he wasn't sure why he trusted that this doctor was telling the truth, but he did. Ric allowed the doctor to place an instrument into his ear and drill through his brain to where the doctor was able to locate the brain worm and extract it. (It sounded a lot like the "bug" that was inserted in Neo's navel in the movie *The Matrix*.)

In any case, Ric said that once the brain worm was out of his head, he could remember who he was, and he thanked the doctor and promptly woke up; for reference, that would have been the night of his second birth-day, January 22, 2010.

Here we were, four days later, listening to this story of what had happened for the first time, and his brother Michael was able to see for himself the interesting phenomena of no short-term memory and the fact that Ric still thought it was 2002. I could see the pained look on Michael's face as Ric asked over and over again, "Where's Dad? Does Dad know what happened to me?"

At one point, the hospital personnel needed us to leave the room so they could clean up Ric and his room. Michael and I stepped out of the room, and Michael said, "You know, we really need to update Ric's memory and tell him that Dad is dead."

I immediately told Michael that no, we did *not* need to do that. Ric was scheduled for surgery the very next day, and there was no way I was going to add even more stress . . . period . . . end of story. I think Michael heard the finality in my voice, saw the look in my eyes, and wisely decided not to argue with me. Lucky for him!

What I didn't share with Michael at the time was that while we'd been at the other facility, Ric kept asking about his dad, and I finally, and hopefully as gently as I could, told Ric that his dad was dead. I saw, felt, and heard the pain that passed through my husband as he experienced his dad's death for the second time.

It was extremely hard on Ric when his father passed away in 2003. He had developed a close and loving relationship with his dad just prior to his father becoming ill and through his father's dying process. I watched Ric as he literally experienced all of that again, only, instead of it taking years, all of that pain, grief, fear, loneliness, and everything else, Ric experienced in just a matter of minutes.

My heart broke for both of them once again. I thought oh, my God, what have I done? I should never have told him; it could have waited.

Literally, as long as it took me to say that to myself and experience my own anguish in empathy, Ric "forgot," and I heard him ask, "So, does my dad know what happened?" Oh, thank God for no short-term memory! You can see why when Michael brought up telling Ric about their dad, I said no way!

After Ric's brother left, I went home as well, but wait—there was *my* journey out of the hospital that night. Of course, I was still so weary and probably a bit bleary, and it was late enough that most of the hospital exits were locked (so no one could get in *or* out).

As I was wandering the halls of this mostly unknown hospital, I happened onto a man who was a little peculiar. I didn't know exactly what was so different about him; he seemed to be a small Asian man with a large grin. I asked if he knew how to get out of the hospital, and he said that we could get out through the emergency room and led me to a door. That was great, except that there was a lock on the door with a number keypad that you had to punch to unlock the door.

It was a solid door, too, so it was impossible to see what was on the other side, and there was no sign on the outside of the door that indicated that it was the back door to the emergency room area. I thought this man might be a hospital employee, but he wasn't dressed like one and he didn't have an identification badge.

When I asked if he worked here, he replied, "Not exactly." What the heck did *that* mean?

I considered knocking on the door and had just raised my hand when the man motioned to me. I could tell that he wanted to say something to me, so I put my hand down and listened. He said, "Eight, eight, three, six, pound." As he was saying each number, then the pound sign, he made a pushing motion with his thumb.

I must have had a quizzical look on my face because he repeated, "Eight, eight, three, six, pound," and repeated the pushing motion with each number.

I realized that he meant that was the code to the lock, but again he didn't have any identifying badge, and he didn't say anything else, even when I asked if it was okay to use the code. I was just so tired, and I wanted to go home, so I thought, what the hell and used the code.

Sure enough, it worked, and I opened the door and walked into a short hallway. The man followed me through the door, and as I got to the end of the hallway, it opened into the emergency room area that was staffed and also had patients. I turned around to thank the man, and he was gone.

He couldn't have passed me, and he didn't go back and out the door we had come in because I would have heard the door open and close. A little freaked out, I turned back around and went through the people in the emergency area, who paid little or no attention to me, and exited the hospital.

It wasn't until I was almost home that I realized the code the man had given me for the door was familiar. Suddenly it hit me that it was the ATM code that my husband and I had shared for the almost nineteen years that we had been together! What are the flipping odds of that?

Once home, I fell into bed and woke early because I knew Ric was being transferred to the hospital in Santa Clara the next morning for surgery.

Tuesday, January 26, 2010

Only a few hours later, I received a call from the hospital telling me that Ric was being loaded into an ambulance for transport, and I hurried to take a shower and get on my way. Michael called me while I was trying to get ready to tell me I needed to get to Santa Clara (big help, this brother-in-law of mine!). To be fair to Michael, I didn't have any patience for anyone except Ric, Chiara, and my mom at that point.

I made it to the hospital in Santa Clara just in time for Ric's arrival. Guess what question the ambulance driver asked me as Ric was unloaded? "Is your husband always like this?"

How I replied this time was "Hard to say. He died. Was resuscitated after 44 minutes of no heartbeat and not breathing. So you tell me, is it possible that he was *ever* like this?"

Describing when Ric first "woke up," I've done my best to convey his enthusiasm when he was talking to his visitors at the hospital even though he "forgot" them immediately upon their departure. What I'm not sure I did was convey how amazingly "normal" Ric would seem in those conversations.

Ric was a consummate salesman. He could sell the proverbial ice to people who already lived in an area surrounded by ice. It was one of his gifts, and it seemed to have traveled through death without any ill effects.

Because of our close relationship prior to his death experience, the fact that I was then pretty much by his side during most of this hospital journey, *and* the fact that I "see" things most people don't, I could tell when he was "selling" versus when he was "really there."

That night after his arrival at the Santa Clara hospital, he was both selling, and he was totally there. This was the night of the <u>Party in Ric's Room</u>. The party list included Ric's brothers, Michael and Len; Len's wife, Peggy; Ric's mother; Ric's daughter Carrie and his son, Kit; our daughter, Chiara; and of course, me.

For more than two hours, Ric was the rock star he had been all of his life, whether he had a guitar in his hand or not. I kept observing from that place of neutrality, and anyone who didn't know what had happened would have thought that there was nothing wrong with him.

The nurses gave us our space, but those who did stop by would do a double take when they looked at Ric's chart, then saw him sitting on the edge of his hospital bed, legs crossed, and entertaining the whole room with stories of his family growing up. Incredible.

Once everyone left, though, I knew it had taken a lot out of him, and soon he forgot that anyone had even been there and that the "party" had taken place! Did I mention that this whole experience was continually challenging me to question my own sanity and grasp on reality?

We both managed some fitful sleep until the early morning hours when the staff came into the room to begin preparing him for the two surgeries.

Wednesday, January 27, 2010

At some point during the time he was at the interim facility, doctors had removed the catheter, and Ric was able to pee into a container. He was still too unsteady on his feet to be able to walk even the short distance to the toilet in his rooms.

From the moment the catheter was removed, I had been helping him with this process. Since his performance the night before had worn him out, I could tell that he would likely be sleeping for a while, which was why I moved out of the chair by his bed and onto a couch in the room to catch some sleep myself.

When the hospital staff came in to prep Ric for surgery, I woke, and the nurse asked, "Where's your husband?"

What? What do you mean, where's my husband?

I quickly jumped up and realized that if the hospital staff member hadn't seen Ric leave the room, the only other option would be that he was in the bathroom. I took a deep breath, praying that I was right, and opened the door to see Ric quietly sitting on the toilet as he asked us both, "What?"

The nurse explained that he didn't have the right color socks to be able to get up and go to the bathroom unassisted. Allow me to explain. Each hospital provided Ric with a number of pairs of socks, and because he was at high risk for falling, he had to wear *red* socks. Since he had an abundance of these socks and I hate wearing shoes, I normally had a pair of them on, too. At each hospital, I was given a brown or gray pair so that I wouldn't be taken for a patient who needed to be told to get back to bed.

Having found my husband and safely delivered him out of the bathroom and back into his bed, the nurse and other staff took blood and began preparing Ric for the procedures.

The first surgery was to insert a stent to open a blockage that they had found in one of his arteries. The other procedure was to insert a defibrillator into his chest. Both surgeries went just fine except for the issue of anesthetic. Ric's tolerance for drugs was quite high, so the anesthesiologist finally had to just put him completely out because he was "awake" and wouldn't stay still for the procedures.

Can't say that I blame the anesthesiologist. On the other hand, doctors were hesitant to put him all the way out lest they would not be able to bring him back to consciousness.

Even with knocking him all the way out, all was well because, again, it wasn't Ric's time to die.

A further note about that ejection fraction—every new doctor who would see Ric would exclaim that he shouldn't be alive based on the percentage for that test. Gosh, what do you say to people who keep telling you that Ric should be dead? I know, right?

The other thing about this journey and me at the hospitals was that I spent quite a bit of time "translating" for medical personnel. What I mean by that is they would talk to Ric about different things, and because, almost from the start, Ric was so coherent when speaking with the medical and support staff, sometimes they wouldn't know what to think.

For example, there was a speech therapist who visited Ric in the hospital at Santa Clara. She was from Napa, where Ric was born and raised. Almost everything that Ric would say, she would look at me, and I would respond, "Yes, that's true," or "No, that's not true."

I found it continually amusing because some of the most unbelievable things that Ric would say would actually be true, and some of the things that seemed most likely were definitely *not* true. You can see why there were many times throughout the week when I was wondering whether I knew what was real and what was not—what was true and what was not.

Just as Ric's time in the various hospitals was one of miracles, magic, and exhaustion as I'm sure you realize from my description thus far, the year following Ric's 44-minute death and coming back to life can be characterized in the same way: a journey of miracles, magic, and exhaustion!

First, let's talk about those Three Reasons.

Chapter 6

The Three Reasons

When Ric was wherever he was when he left his body, he had the ability to see *everything*, literally, including everything from his past. There are stories of people who were dying or thought they were facing death, such as mountain climbers who were falling, when everything that had ever happened to them flashed before their eyes.

This is called a "panoramic life review," and this was the case with Ric. There was also something else that happened—Ric could also see forward in "time." He explained that in this place of "eternity," if you will, there was no time. Everything was in that eternal moment.

In my imagination, when Ric was "up there," he could certainly see and feel the connection with me and his daughter and with everyone he loved and who loved him. Thus, the First Reason, love and family, inspired Ric to come back to his life here on earth.

Yet, when you're in eternity and you're in *unconditional* love, there just isn't anything better! As Dr. Deepak Chopra says, "There is no power stronger than love." While Ric could feel the love of those he'd left behind, he wasn't completely compelled to do anything about it because he was already immersed in eternal and unconditional *Love*.

As for the Second Reason, music, certainly that was extraordinary and a thread that kept Ric going through many challenging times during his life. Music and playing the guitar gave him a focus in his teen years that was more intense than sports or even girls. He reveled in the years he spent on the road as a rock musician, even having Van Halen open for Ric's band!

Throughout any disappointments and challenging times, music was always there to soothe his soul and lighten his heart. An integral part of his very being is music, and that, too, while quite compelling, especially when considered with the First Reason, still wasn't enough to make him decide, to make him choose, to come back.

In this space of being able to see literally everything every *where* and every-*when*, somewhere along the line, Ric's antennae picked up the fact that for the first time in 52 years, the San Francisco Giants baseball team was going to win the World Series in 2010 (the year of Ric's death and resurrection).

Ric had been a *fan* since the Giants moved from New York to San Francisco in May of 1957. Ric was just six years old when that happened, and with the team now in his own back yard, so to speak, he took ownership of his love for baseball and, in particular, the San Francisco Giants.

Ric, his beloved father, and Ric's brother Len went to as many games as possible during the time he was growing up. When Ric realized that for the first time since his team had moved to San Francisco they were going to win the World Series—oh my God—that was it. That was the kicker. In this netherworld of death, Ric determined, "I am going back!"

Hey, I thought this might be a good time to introduce myself. I'm Ric Adamo. Yeah, I'm the dead guy. I also thought it would be a good idea to let Bev tell you most of the story to this point, but now that we're into the reasons, my Three Reasons, for coming back to this life, I think it's time that you actually heard from me.

This Reason #1—love, family, yadda yadda yadda—well, let me tell ya, I don't think it was a reason I recognized for a lot of my life, and here's why—I was an asshole. I know . . . Some of you out there who know me might find that hard to believe (ha-ha), but still, I was, and it took this experience to teach me what love is.

I knew that I loved my daughter. I loved her from the moment she was born. I actually got to hold her before Bev did because Chiara was born through a C-section, so I got to hold her while Bev was in the recovery room. I got to take her to get cleaned up and have her first tests done, and boy, did she scream when they poked her heel to take some blood. She wasn't liking that whatsoever.

Yeah, I completely fell in love with my daughter Chiara from the moment that she actually even came to be.

I'd known Bev was pregnant before she knew she was. It wasn't anything we were thinking about, having kids. Well, at least, I wasn't. I already had two grown children and a granddaughter. Didn't think I needed anybody else.

But then, when I could tell Bev was pregnant, I just knew it was meant to be. So, yes, I did fall in love with my daughter, but that doesn't mean I still wasn't an asshole, sometimes even to her.

In case you were wondering, asshole is my word for myself, and you'll hear me call myself that again. I've heard Bev call me that during the more than twenty years of our relationship and marriage, but still, it's what I recognize myself to be a lot of times.

Before I go on about this love thing, this family thing, let me tell you a about me and what it was like for me when I first came back.

I would very much like to say that I was just a normal guy, but I'm not! I am, however, a self-centered, egotistical, hateful, fearful, lying asshole who has never forgiven anyone who did me wrong. I've hurt and disappointed many people—with no remorse or guilt whatsoever. Maybe that is normal. I certainly am not someone who could say. It seemed fairly normal while I was living through it.

I've been gifted with some athletic ability, musical ability, salesmanship, and an entrepreneur's spirit. I was blessed with three beautiful children. Although I was married four times, all of my close friends have always said that all my wives were nice people; they just hated me. Yes, I've had some good friends and am still close to most of my friends who are still alive, but they seem to be getting fewer every day.

As a child of the '50s, I had a great childhood with baseball, fishing, swimming, biking, and dirt, lots of dirt, my mother always said, and two brothers to get dirty with.

As a teen of the '60s in the San Francisco Bay Area . . . Okay, okay, I know they say if you remember the '60s, you weren't there, but I have to say, it was great! Music, drugs, and cute little hippy girls—and, believe me, I enjoyed all I could.

The '70s, '80s, and '90s kind of turned into a time of sex, drugs, rock-n-roll, and lots of travel, playing music and later as a salesman.

There's a lot more I could say about these times of my life, but it would take a whole book, so maybe another time. This brings us to the last twenty-five years and the things that led to the "event."

I met Bev for the first time on October 4, 1991, when we were both flying from California to Colorado to sell pianos. Immediately when I first saw this tall, long-legged blonde beauty walking down the aisle on the plane, I thought, nope! Never gonna happen that she'll sit next to me! When she did, I remember thinking that I had just under a couple of hours to see if I could sell her on at least a one-night stand. I've always been damn good at sales!

Okay, hold on just a minute! I'd like to go on record that when I found out that the fat Italian macho man who happened to be sitting in the seat next to mine on the plane, was also the infamous Ric Adamo, top piano salesman in the company, I knew immediately that this wasn't going to be the fun and interesting trip I'd thought it might be!

I was the worst salesperson in the company, and I guess

the owner thought it would be interesting to see what would happen if the two of us worked a show together. I learned later that it was one of Ric's sales buddies who had made the request for me to join them because *he* thought it would be interesting to see what happened between Ric and me.

While I could tell Ric was interested in me, it was dislike at first sight, as far as I was concerned, and it didn't get better as the flight and then the week of working together, went on.

Ric asked me out probably a total of ten times before I finally gave in and spent a miserable evening listening to him go on and on about how great he was while watching him drink scotch (I don't drink alcohol), eat veal parmesan (I am a vegetarian), and swear like a sailor (not that I couldn't; I just didn't care for foul language).

The worst part of it was that he kept trying to tell me that he "played guitar." Yeah, right. I had just ended a long relationship with a "real" guitar player who was incredibly talented and had a band for many years.

When we returned to California, Ric still kept calling and inviting me over to hear him with *his* band. I finally said yes just to shut him up. I'm sure you can see what's coming. When I got to his house, I could hear the band warming up, and as I walked into the garage where they were just beginning a song, Ric launched into a guitar solo that melted my heart and touched my soul. The rest, as they say, is history. We were married on June 13, 1992.

He-he-he. The moment I saw Bev step into the garage, I played that guitar like I knew how. When I saw those beautiful green eyes of hers get really big, I said to myself, Gotcha! As Bev just said, the rest is history.

I only want to tell you a few things about those years. I spent most of this time working, traveling, and just doing what most people do to live in this world. Okay, I spent a *lot* of time working, so I didn't take time to pay much attention to the people and world around me. It was, however, stressful and took most of my time.

There were some perks, like free travel, and most of my co-workers were great to be around and said that I was one of the best at what I did. In 1999, I decided to open my own business to stop all the travel and stress of working for someone else. Little did I know that having your own small business can be as stressful, if not more so, than working for someone else. Nobody had told me that!

Anyway, I spent ten years being mostly successful and experiencing the perks and pitfalls of being my own boss. At the end of this time, I found myself sitting at my desk, not liking my life too much. A great day was when nobody bugged me, so I could play video games, listen to baseball on the computer, and smoke.

My favorite lunch was two double-doubles with cheese, fries, and a chocolate shake from In-N-Out, then I would go home, sit in front of the TV, and eat more, totally losing my mind in worthless stuff on the tube.

During this time, if I'd had the connections, I would have turned to drugs and drink again, but I'd lost these connections many years earlier and hadn't been drinking either for many years, so I just stuffed my face and went on. I was unhappy and unhealthy.

I was feeling like maybe my life didn't have any purpose. What the hell was I here for anyway? Every day seemed like the same old story, and I didn't see a point to the story! By December of 2006, I weighed in at 350 pounds or more and, of course, I was still smoking cigarettes, not to mention the occasional cigar.

Even after losing a hundred pounds by 2007, I seem to remember something about the odds of being dead within five years after the diagnosis of congestive heart failure, and my guess is that my heart had started failing years before I was diagnosed.

January 20, 2010 was pretty much a normal day. We, my family and I, had plans for that night. We were going to a club to listen to some friends play the blues. We all got seated and the music got going and right in the middle of the first or second song, I can't remember, I died. Cardiac arrest stopped my heart, and that was

71

that!

At this point, I would like to say to my wife, daughter, and mother-in-law, I'm sorry. I have no idea what that must have been like for them to see me die right in front of them. You've read the story written by my wife Bev because the next days were an odyssey only she could tell. What she went through was way beyond my ability, and probably most people's, to understand.

For days, I was either dead or in a coma, and she was there the whole time. For the next six months, I truly wasn't there. Plus, I wasn't a very nice person during the recovery.

What she did during this time was amazing. I'd like to say that love, kindness, patience, and understanding were easy for her because of what an incredible person she is, but it wasn't, and even with all her wonderful gifts she shares with all the people around her, there's no amount of thanks that I can give to cover the cost.

My daughter Chiara and mother-in-law JoAn were pretty darn wonderful themselves although with a little less patience, but always with love.

Ciao,

Ric

Chapter 7

Reason #1 – Love

So a little more about Reason #1—love and family.

Recall the scene of Ric's second birth-day when the doctor came in to see if Ric really was awake and knew his own name, my name, and Chiara's name. A couple of things about this. The first is that Ric never lost himself. He came back knowing who he was, Ric Adamo, knowing that I was his wife, and knowing that Chiara was, without a doubt, his daughter.

That connection was so strong for both of them. I believe that was why Chiara was vibrating at such an intensity in the café when Ric's soul left his body.

It's almost as if the connection between Chiara and her dad was palpable such that when his spirit left his body, when we were at the jazz café, Chiara was still connected to his spirit and vice versa, meaning that he, too, was at a high vibration. When you're only spirit, you're totally at a high vibration. Because of that, Chiara in her physical form was vibrating so intensely. It was phenomenal to witness.

Chiara also had an unfailing belief that her dad was going to recover from his death, no matter what the doctors said and no matter what the tests showed. Of course, she loved her dad with all her heart, yet this "knowing" of hers seemed to be "other worldly" when I look back on it. The love between the two of them was, and is, humbling and inspiring.

Chiara was just finishing her first half-year as a freshman in high school, and both she and her dad were excited about the fact that Chiara would be playing tennis for her high school team. Chiara had picked up a racket when she was five years old and had never put it down. She was an awesome player and a "leftie," which made her even more special and desirable for the team.

Ric had always been her biggest fan; however, during the months of his recovery and after, supporting Chiara and her love of tennis seemed even more important for Ric. He became the mainstay of her world, both in terms of her academics and her tennis, which was perfect, since it turned out that I would be busy supporting the family financially and making sure Ric was able to get the medical care he needed to continue on his road to recovery

The other thing that I've already noted is that when Ric identified me as "my wife," what I found to be absolutely hilarious is that he wasn't quite sure which wife I was. This was a man who had been married four times.

At the time, I found it funny, and during the first time we were together after his spirit returned and he was talking with me, he did confuse me a couple of times with one of his other wives (as I already shared with you). Most of the time, he knew I was Bev, aka Babe. He was able to identify with that.

There were a few times when we were talking, he would say something, and I would ask, "Who am I?" He would say the name of one of his other wives. I didn't take offense at the time. Again, I found it amusing, and now, I simply find it miraculous that he came back at all, and the conversations we had, I found endearing and so special.

He spoke of music and baseball and the fact that he knew Chiara and me when the doctor had asked him. He told me that there were three reasons he'd come back. The First Reason was definitely his daughter and, I'd like to think, me. Ric has always said that Chiara is his miracle and I'm his miracle maker. Very sweet.

I know Ric wrote that he didn't know much about love, and I would have to say that's probably true in one sense, yet when we met, he told me that he would never leave our marriage and that if I decided that this relationship wasn't for me, then I would need to be the one who would leave.

Funny thing is, at one point, I did think that was what I wanted, yet at the time, it seemed like way too much trouble to get a divorce. I decided that since I obviously couldn't change Ric, I would work on myself instead. I redoubled my efforts at being a better person, expanding my spiritual, mental, and emotional self.

Ric talks about the love, patience, kindness, and understanding that I exhibited throughout this experience and the time of recovery afterward; however, it was because he loved me so much that he told me he would never leave me, coupled with the fact that I thought it was just too much trouble to get a divorce, that I began the journey into myself and becoming that person who is love, patience, kindness, and understanding.

What's even more interesting to me is that at the time I turned my attention from trying to change Ric to changing myself, everyone around me also seemed to change. As I already mentioned, funny thing, right?

Coming Back Home

Bev was driving me home from the hospital in Santa Clara where they'd put in a stent and a pacemaker. I had no knowledge of these events nor anything else that had gone on, and I just barely knew that it was Bev driving. When I would look at the freeway and the towns we were going through, I could remember some of it, but not a lot, though I had driven these roads many times.

Bev got me home and sat me down in a chair. I can't describe the fear I was feeling. I didn't know where I was, who I was, or who the people around me were. I didn't know my address, phone number, what town I was in, what food I liked or disliked. I was in a lot of pain. My chest and ribs hurt so bad I could barely move. I was told later it was from the CPR and paddles that they'd used to help bring me back.

I sat there, doing and saying nothing, then Chiara came home from school, and I finally began to figure out that she was such a strong energy in my life that just her presence could make me feel great. As Bev told you, her role in my return is absolutely a miracle.

Most of the time, even now, I'm still a long way from normal, but over the next couple of weeks after my return home, things started to get better—and worse. Better because I was beginning to be able to talk and breathe. My chest was getting better, so I could at least move, yet I wasn't treating my family very well.

I've never been a good patient, and all I wanted to do was get away from those people who kept holding me back. I truly believed they were lying to me about everything and doing all they could to confuse me at every turn, so I would just keep smiling and nodding, but hiding what I was really suspecting.

It was a little freaky because it felt like what I'd experienced many decades earlier, when I'd had a bad trip on LSD as a teen, full of paranoia, fear, and violent actions to the people around me. Yeah, it was bad. I know a lot of this, so far, sounds like the rambling of a mad man, but I continued in this state of fear, paranoia, and suspicion for the next few months.

When Ric and I decided to write this book, I wrote my part of the story, and he wrote his. We never really talked to each other about what each of us was writing. It wasn't until after I had finished "my story" that I read what Ric had written.

There were some things that surprised me, and the fear that he talks about here was one of them. While I could sense something deeper under the anger and hostility, and even physical pain, I had no idea of the depth of the fear that Ric lived with when he got back to earth. I could tell that some of his "filters" were no longer there and that he had even less patience now than before he'd died.

I seemed to have gained the patience he lost, however, and that was a good thing. While I don't think I could have been more patient with Ric during the time of his recovery, I wonder if I could have done something more to ease the mental anguish he was in.

The thing about Reason #1, love and family, is that when Ric came back physically surrounded by this unconditional love, I experienced an amazing and life-changing transformation myself. As I've already shared, I have always felt "connected" with Source, God, the Universe whatever word or words that might be used to refer to that omnipotent power/being that created us.

The actual physical experience of this "presence" that Ric literally brought back with him was beyond words. Over the next year of recovery with Ric, this unconditional love experience continued to fuel me and to subtly, and not so subtly, change me.

Chapter 8

Reason #2 – Music

Reason #2 in this case was something that literally made Ric's heart and guitar—sing! Ric came back into this life to work with his blues band partner, Marshal Kee, to record their original and cover versions of songs for their CD. Marshal, as you'll recall, was one of the first people to show up at the hospital. He was also one of the first people to visit Ric at our home once we were back.

Everything is truly connected. When Ric died, we were in a jazz club listening to music. When Ric came back, one of the things I was so afraid of was that he wouldn't be able to play his guitar. He'd been playing guitar since he was a teenager. He made money by teaching guitar. He was in a band throughout most of his life. He even won a battle of the bands in high school in a hometown festival.

When he was older, Ric travelled around the country playing rock and roll. When he first came back and wasn't able to use his fine motor skills (he had to be fed because he couldn't pick up a spoon or fork to get the food from the plate to his mouth), it was super scary. All I could think of was what his quality of life would be without his music, without his being able to play the guitar.

Amazingly, his motor skills came back incredibly quickly while he was still in the hospital after he came out of the coma. Again, this was another miracle.

I was sitting there like a total veg, but I couldn't stop recycling all the info in my mind. Some people may call this a "life review," but it was more like a tornado of information going so fast that I couldn't grab anything. All I could do was sit there and smile, nod, and be scared and paranoid about everything and everybody around me.

It was day seven of my return home, I think, when all of a sudden, I got a hold of something. "I'm a guitar player." I started reaching for this, but it was like falling off a cliff and hanging onto a branch so small I just knew that I was going to fall. I have no idea how long this went on, but it seemed like a lifetime.

Finally, I got up and walked into my music room, which, until this time, I hadn't even remembered existing. I sat down, picked up my guitar, and started to play. My mother-in-law, JoAn, walked in and had those big eyes watching me with total disbelief. She said I was playing just like I always had and that it was amazing.

For my part, the tornado of my thoughts began to slow down; the music was restoring my mind to that moment in time, the present. As I played and listened to the music, I could feel the vibration of the strings through my body. Each note seemed to pull a little more info out. At one point, I started to cry, then I would laugh, but I just kept playing and healing. It was intense.

I eventually had to stop, so I got up and left the room and sat down. In that moment, even with all the pain, I fell asleep and for the first time, actually rested. I've always believed that the blues could save the world, and now, I believe it saved me.

When I returned home and my mom told me that Ric had been playing his guitar and had sounded just like he always did, I was astounded. Later, when I asked him to play something for me and he did, it was amazing.

Thirty days after he'd died, he played his first gig in Sacramento, then another gig back at the Main Street Jazz

Café. For me, returning to the jazz café with Ric and Marshal on stage was surreal. How could it be possible? Thirty days previously, that man was dead, and now he's up on stage playing his songs as though nothing had happened. It was astounding.

I did my best to hang on. I started to want nothing more than to play a gig with Marshal. After I got home from the hospital, I asked him to watch the Super Bowl with me, so we could make a plan. He said he would, so I had something to look forward to.

An amazing thing happened on the same Super Bowl Sunday. My son, Kit, came to see me with his new baby girl, Camille. When I held her in my arms, I felt such love I almost couldn't breathe. The life in her was so new, pure, and beautiful that I came to realize that just maybe I had a chance at a new life also.

Marshal and I figured that the best time to play would be Taco Tuesdays at Kim's Country Kitchen in Lincoln, California. We were already booked for the show before I had died, so it would be perfect. Now, I just had to convince Bev that I could do it. It took some fast-talking, but we did it.

I began playing my guitar a lot more, going through our

sets, because we would be playing for four sets, and with setup and tear down, it would take about six hours.

I'm not one to say that there was Divine intervention going on, but something was driving me. There's no way I should have been able to do this. I can't say I remember a lot of what went on, but I'll tell you what I think happened and the things Marshal told me later.

Somehow, I remembered how to set up my equipment and get ready to play. The place was packed—I mean standing room only. I had played at Kim's many times, so I knew most of the staff and fans who'd come to see us, but that night, as I looked out at the crowd, I didn't see anyone I knew.

This was frightening, so I just looked at Marshal and concentrated on the music. At our break, Marshal said I was doing great and to just relax. I went into the crowd and started saying hello and smiling. I was getting lots of hugs and well wishes from all around, but I still didn't recognize anyone.

Here began the dialogue that I adopted when people asked questions about what happened.

"I'm doing great, thanks."

"What was it like being dead?"

"I don't know. I was dead!"

This got me by for most everybody, and I just got back to playing my guitar. I should say, "hiding behind my guitar," because it was all the protection I had besides Marshal.

When the third set ended, I was about to collapse, so I called Bev and asked if she could come and get me. I had originally planned on staying one more night with Marshal, but I knew I couldn't make it. She agreed, so we went into the fourth set, and from all accounts, I played great. Everybody said it was the best set of the night. I just wish I hadn't been so exhausted.

I got home, and it took a week to recover, but I did and was ready for the next gig.

Ric's relationship with his band partner, Marshal, was very, very special. It wasn't only that they had a musical partnership; they were also best friends. When Ric's dad died in 2003, Ric grew close to Marshal. They had known each other for years in the piano sales business in which both of them had been involved for decades. Ric and Marshal talked about a lot of things that Ric would have talked to his dad about. It was great to see.

It was time for another gig, this time at the Main Street Jazz Café. This was the scene of the event, and as it turned out, it was exactly thirty days from the day I'd dropped dead on their floor.

The place was packed and overflowing onto the street. Most of my family, friends, and friends of Crossroads were there. It was amazing. Marshall and I started playing, and we just burned the house down for four hours. It was great.

Some of the people there were Mark and Paul, the two guys who'd done CPR on me, Joel the bartender who helped the EMTs, the owners of the club, Ken and Joe, and others, too many to name. These folks were there for me at the club and at the hospital for Bev, and I can't thank them enough.

I'm sure Bev will say a lot more about these people, so I'll move on.

What can I say about the amazing people who didn't hesitate to jump in and help Ric that night? They're heroes and have my most profound respect and gratitude. My heart is full, yet I find that words are not enough to describe that gratitude. My thanks are inadequate to recognize them.

Please know that my simple "thank you" is my wish for

them to always have their hearts' desires and the best of everything!

After that gig, we were outside of the jazz club, cooling off and talking about how the night went. Even then and there we felt an inspiration. I'm not even sure who had the idea first, but someone decided that this music needed to be recorded. Not only the cover tunes, but also the original music that Ric and Marshal had written, either as individuals or as a team.

Oh, by the way, did I happen to mention that Marshal had cancer? He wasn't a completely well man himself. Here were these two old guys, barely clinging to life, playing and singing their hearts out. It was awesome to see and hear! Loved it! Every single note of it! They were damn good!

Marshal was getting worse, as was my friend Howard, whom I had worked with in the piano business for decades. I couldn't get over them both being sick at the same time. Marshal was still able to play on Fridays, so I went up whenever I could to help out.

It might sound like too routine of a life, but it was how I kept on some kind of course to stay sane doing the same thing, day after day. It was how I believed I could feel okay.

One of the hardest things about wanting to play music again was that it was so hard finding people to play with. Marshal was 61, and I was 60. Not bad for two guys who probably shouldn't have made it to 30 . . .

When all my days seemed to be the same, I knew I needed to get out. In October 2011, I decided to head back to the mountains for the last weekend of trout season. I went to see Marshal on Friday at Kim's before heading out. He told everyone that this was his last time to play.

As usual, he played and sang great. He brought tears to the whole joint. We packed him up, and I returned home to pack for the mountains.

I left on Tuesday and spent Wednesday and Thursday walking through the forest, catching trout, and thinking. It was calming. I thought I either needed to spend more time in the mountains or I should just move there and be done with it.

My dad had done just that. He spent most of his last three years at the cabin in Hat Creek, mostly by himself. I can only imagine what had been going through his mind during that time, but I went to see him a lot, and he really did seem to be at peace.

When I got back home, Marshal had been put in a "home," but he couldn't stand it, so they brought him back to his home where he was more comfortable. On the Saturday after he returned home, I spent the day with him and let his wife have a day off to do things that needed to be done.

We talked, I played guitar for him, and we watched a ball game. He said he thought he was ready to go, and I told him that God may not give us angel wings after the lives we had lived, but he surely would let us play in the band with a harp with golden strings.

Two days later, Marshall passed. I was sad to have lost my best friend, but also happy his pain was over. It was hard to watch first my father, then Marshal, two really strong men, wither away in pain; it's not good for the soul. And I'm still searching for something. I'm just not sure what.

The experience of recording their CD was extraordinary for both Ric and Marshal, and the product—the songs, the music, the CD—is amazing. During the course of all this, although Ric continued to "get better," Marshal's health deteriorated, until finally he was at the point where Marshal was obviously dying and getting ready to pass over. Ric and I were inspired to write a song, "When the Angels Sing."

When Ric returned home from one of his visits to Marshal's and told me about his inspiration for the song, he also said that he needed my help because I'm a songwriter and have been writing songs for a long time. When Ric asked me to do this, I knew that it was going to be a collaborative effort between Ric, Marshal, and me.

I didn't have to have them in the room with me when I wrote the song. I didn't even need any more than the one line Ric had given me, "when the angels sing." I could feel both Ric and Marshal with me as the words just seemed to flow out of me and onto the paper. The melody flowed out of my mouth as I sang the words.

Beverly Adamo

When the Angels Sing

By Ric and Bev Adamo

For Marshal Kee & All Musicians

Time to move on down the trail
Take my walk through the mystery veil
Leave behind my cares, my troubles, and my pain
Just take my spirit when I go
And there's one thing you need to know
That there's music in my soul, and this I pray

(Dear Lord) When I die and the Angels sing,
You don't have to give me a pair of those wings.
Give me a harp with golden strings
When I die and the Angels sing

Lived my life the best I could
Trying to do all the things that I should
And mistakes I often made along the way
But judge me not on how I lived,
Look instead at the joy I spread
With the music that I love and that I play

CHORUS
GUITAR SOLO

I see the light, and I'm going home,
So don't be sad, just sing along

And be grateful for this song, we sing and pray

CHORUS
ENDING

When I die and the Angels sing

Acapella

When I die . . . and the Angels . . . are singing the blues . . .
(When the Angels sing)

Ric was able to play and sing this to Marshal before Marshal passed away. At Marshal's celebration of life, Ric also played his guitar and sang this song to his friend as a way of saying, "See you in a while."

Chapter 9

Reason #3 – The San Francisco Giants

I was still having bouts of anger and rage along with paranoia. A lot of the anger came from the ups and downs due to smoking—I was supposed to have quit, but I didn't want to.

I kept putting myself through withdrawal by smoking for three days when no one was around, then when people would be home, I couldn't smoke. Of course, I'd go crazy.

I decided to throw myself into three different things. First, tennis. I started watching tennis on TV, so I could learn as much as I could to help Chiara with her game.

Second, music. I started practicing more, and we had gigs, so this was good.

Third, baseball. Being a lifelong San Francisco Giants fan, this was a great year to watch or listen to every game. I mean—they won the World Series! It can't get much better than that.

Now if you're not a sports fan, you might be saying to yourself, "You've got to be kidding me! The love of his family and the music that he was here to produce for the world weren't compelling enough reasons to come back, but silly baseball games, even a team winning the World Series was the biggest reason he came back?"

I wouldn't say it was the biggest reason, yet it was icing on the cake. One of the best things that I learned throughout this experience and the process of Ric's death and miraculous rebirth, is *yes*, I have *my* Three Reasons as well.

Everyone has their own *Three Reasons* for living, and they're things that are deep, profound, and world-changing. Without that icing on the cake, without that "kicker," without that fun, that "just for the pure hell of it" excitement factor, life can be pretty damn boring when you're just so profound all the frickin' time!

One of the things that I absolutely love about the Dalai Lama, Eckhart Tolle, and some of the other awesomely spiritual people who have blessed this planet is that they don't take themselves too seriously. They have a great sense of humor and joy. They laugh. They can see the fun and joy in things.

When it comes to baseball and Ric, that was *his* joy that had no "useful function," a joy that could not be, and frankly did not need to be, justified. A joy that was simply important because it was *joy*. There didn't have to be any deeper meaning to it.

Going through that 2010 season and series, with the San Francisco Giants and with Ric, was magical and miraculous. We watched every single baseball game because this was one of the changes that happened with Ric. He went from being a Giants "fan of sorts," to eating, breathing, and living the SF Giants.

You see, he used to go to the Giants games when he was a young boy with his dad and younger brother, but prior to Ric's death, baseball hadn't seemed to be that important to him. Yeah, he'd been interested, but he could take it or leave it as to whether he watched the games or followed the Giants too closely.

Before he'd died, it was football, football, football, and when he came back, it was baseball, baseball, baseball. Hmmmm, isn't that interesting? As a matter of fact, Ric had been released from the hospital in time for the 2010 Super Bowl game, but I'm not sure that he even really watched it. Marshal was over, and Ric's newborn granddaughter also paid a visit. There's that echo of love, family, and music, right?

We watched every single Giants game. Halfway through the season, I was sitting there on the couch, watching the Giants, who weren't doing all that great at the time, and I had this epiphany. I looked at the Giants game, the players there on the television screen, looked over at my husband, and into the air and said to myself, "Oh, my God! The Giants are going to win the World Series!"

It's too bad I'm not a betting woman because had I made some substantial wagers at that time during the season, that the Giants would win it all, I could have walked away a wealthy woman, but alas, I didn't do that.

Instead, I simply allowed myself to experience the amazing truth of the moment. No matter the struggle and "torture" that all the other Giants fans were experiencing during that season, I knew the Giants were going to win. It didn't matter what the situation looked like in any of the games. During the playoff and World Series, I knew what the end result was going to be.

I know I'm writing about some pretty serious shit here, and just so you don't get the idea that I was a serious guy, my sense of humor, while not always appreciated by Bev, was still going strong.

I don't want you to think that I was the only crazy one in the family either before *or* after I died, so I asked Bev to tell you what she did during that 2010 Giants season to "help the Giants win." Here's how she responded.

Oh, the promises you make when you love someone! I told Ric I would tell you about this. As I already said, if I had *truly* believed that the Giants winning the World Series was a done deal, I wouldn't have had to do this. It's interesting how superstitious people can be when it comes to sports and winning games.

I was wondering if there was anything that I could "do" during the 2010 season to help the Giants win. I got my answer loud and clear one Friday morning.

Every other morning on my daily commute, I'd get into my car, and before starting it and heading off to my job, I would roll my freshly washed and dried hair onto big rollers so that by the time I reached my destination, my hair would have a nice curl in it that lasted for two days.

I didn't know whether or not other people in the cars on the highway noticed that my hair was in rollers. For the most part, probably not, and even if they did, it was unlikely that I knew them.

One Friday, a day that was supposed to be a non-roller day, my hair had a few ends sticking up, so I decided that I had time to put the rollers in my hair before I started to work. I didn't just put a couple of rollers where my hair was the worst; I rolled every single strand of my hair onto twenty large rollers all over my head.

As I reached to turn the key in the car ignition, it hit me that I absolutely had to stop and put gas in my car before I left town. Waiting until I reached my destination just wouldn't work. I could either take out all the rollers and put them back in after I got the gas, or I could just pump the gas "as is."

I probably could have gone to the highest priced gas station where no one else was buying gas and parked at the very farthest pump so no one would have noticed me. It's not in me to pay any more for gas than I have to, so I went to my usual station that had more than sixteen pumps and was always busy.

I pulled into the only open pump that was at the end, jumped out of the car, and began taking all the steps involved in putting gas in my car. Of course, I was feeling extremely self-conscious, so I looked around to see if anyone was paying attention to me.

Not only was almost everyone noticing me, they were standing on tiptoes and leaning around the pumps so that they could get a good look at this roller-haired wonder who just popped up in their midst. I mustered a smile, and, finally, one of the spectators called out, "Nice hair!"

From someplace deep within my soul, I heard a response starting to build, and to my surprise (and likely the surprise of everyone there), I responded in a loud voice, "Why, thank you! I'm helping the Giants win the World Series this year!"

After a moment of stunned silence, every one of those folks (including those who originally missed my entrance) started smiling even bigger and nodding in understanding.

Without missing a beat, I continued, "Every other day for the entire season, I'm wearing these rollers in my hair, and I think that's why the Giants are gonna win the Series this year!"

A brave soul, without a hair on his head said quite loudly, "Where can I get some of those?" All eyes turned to him with incredulous looks on their faces, as he added, "For my wife, of course!"

Go Giants!

I know that those hair rollers really didn't do the trick as the deciding factor for the World Series win. It was a wild and Divine combination of connections and people that simply, courageously, and awesomely led to that win, and Ric really did "see" that all of those connections were coming together to result in that World Series victory.

I could feel it "through" Ric (although he didn't seem to

have the same awareness of what was going to happen as I did, but at the time, he still didn't think anything had happened while he was dead). Before you see that this was very far from the truth, it's time to hear more from Ric about his yearlong journey back through the veil of death into his new life.

Chapter 10

More Miracles, Magic & Exhaustion

Chapter Note: This chapter outlines Ric's road to recovery that has been an ongoing experience for Ric and our family since 2010.

Now begins the comeback trail. Right now, looking back, it doesn't seem like it was very long or bumpy, but at the time, I never thought it would end.

2010

For the first six months after his death, Ric wasn't allowed to drive. This is California law for anyone who has lost consciousness. In the first place, I wasn't sure that he was all the way "there." He was good at selling, and that included selling others that he was just fine.

Being so emotionally intimate with him and being around him all the time, I could tell there were other things going on and that he was close to "losing it" at any moment. He had "lost" some of the filters and all of the "very little" patience that he had once possessed.

I started thinking how trapped I was. They took my driver's license away and wouldn't let me smoke. Plus, I had to eat just special stuff. I truly felt that it was a conspiracy to make my life miserable. Now, I know it all was for my own good, but it was tough, so in my wee little mind I thought that if I could sneak around and do some of those things, I would be so happy.

When they finally left me alone, I would get my magnet key from the wheel well on my truck, which no one knew was there, and drive to the store and get smokes and anything else I felt I deserved. Keep in mind that the little store in our neighborhood was only four blocks away, and that was a good thing because it was all I could do, but I sure showed them.

Oh, holy moly! Had I known about this, I'm not sure what I would have done. As a parent, I know that there are things that my daughter has done that I'm better off *not* knowing and that I trust were things that she just had to do. Obviously, they resulted in her being the amazing and awesome young lady she is today.

I know there were many things I did, more out of naiveté and ignorance rather than rebellion or spite, from which I learned valuable life lessons and that my parents (as far as I can tell) never knew about.

I believe we all have "guardian angels" who are meant to help us through some things like that, and I know that this was the case with Ric. I wasn't meant to know about his escapades until long after the fact, and if they helped Ric move through the fear he expressed, gave him motivation to live, and "showed" us, then blessed be!

After about two months, my motor skills were doing really well. I was playing guitar, driving, etc. The big thing was I couldn't read too well. I mean I could read, but I couldn't remember what I read.

The psych people said I was doing great, but they had no idea how long it would be or if I would get all the way back to full brain functioning. My percent of brain functioning was still kinda low, but I told them after all the fun I'd had in my life, I was lucky to have ten percent, and that's most likely more than I had anyway.

Around this time, the fun began. They hooked me up with a psychologist and a speech therapist to check out my brain functions. Of course, I charmed all of them into believing I was fine. I took all their tests, did all my homework, and went to all my appointments, and they finally let me loose after a few months.

Bev, however, knew better. She was still seeing the fits of rage that seemed totally uncontrollable and scared the whole family. I will say that I wasn't physical, but verbally, I was much like a male gorilla protecting his territory. My rage was loud and fast. In the case of fight or flight, I'm a fighter, and I believed I was under a never-ending attack from everyone around me.

A quick word about all the doctor appointments and tests. I'm so grateful for the doctors and technicians! There were so many appointments and trips to this facility or that, it was a blur yet, at the same time, each appointment still stands out in my memory. I not only transported Ric to all of these rendezvous, I also was there with him during the appointments and tests.

I already spoke of the "translating" I did in the hospital and also helping the professionals sort out what was real and what was not. I was doing a lot of the same during these sessions.

What I found both disconcerting and amusing was that I was "taking the tests" along with Ric, and this man who had died and come back was scoring a lot higher on many of the tests than I was! I immediately went home from one of the first appointments and opened an account on luminosity.com, and while I told Ric that it was for him to do mind/memory exercises, I certainly spent as much time as I could on the site for my brain.

After about four months, I'm starting to feel pretty good. There were some problems, but for the most part, my body seemed to be recovering. The docs were happy with my progress. Of course, I had to eat a special diet and take about forty pills a day, including vitamins and supplements.

My mind felt kinda locked up. I couldn't remember small things, like how my computer worked. I couldn't remember passwords or how to get in and out of programs. This was frustrating because I still felt trapped with no freedom, like all I had left was mindless TV.

At this point, I need to say that something was going on spiritually with me. I kept feeling there was some missing part that I wasn't getting.

I would wonder, did something happen when I died and I just can't remember? What *did* happen? Better stop trying to get it. Maybe it will come to me. Just want to get over feeling like I'm missing something.

After five months, though things were still a little crazy, I seemed to be getting better more and more each day. I still felt trapped, but I was down to a month until I could get my license back, which, in my mind, was going to free me up to live again.

I had just been told about remapping brain paths, and I think that was what was going on. It seems the brain will make a new road around the damaged areas to access stored info. It seemed to be working because lots of stuff started coming back and still is today.

This remapping of brain paths was actually something we happened upon during a frustrating experience, which we then began using consciously over the course of the next six months. Here's what happened. Ric called me, and I could tell that he was at the end of his (at that time) short rope of patience. Even though I was at work, attempting to catch up and focus, I always did my best to make time if Ric called or needed anything, so when I saw him pop up on my phone, I answered immediately.

Ric told me that he was looking for a physical file folder in which he had a document containing needed information. There weren't that many files in my husband's home office, so worst-case scenario, I could look through every file to find what he was looking for (I was the one with the patience, as I kept reminding myself).

Ric wanted to find the file immediately! My intuition told me not to travel a straight line or logical way of finding this file. I had to figure out what *that* meant.

When I'm looking for an answer, I always ask a question. In this case, I asked Ric, "What is the information you're looking for?"

He said it had something to do with a specific piano sale.

"Do you remember the sale? Do you remember what the person looked like who bought the piano?"

I'm sure that he wasn't expecting me to ask that, so he paused and said that he could remember what the person looked like, but not his name—that was what he was looking for. I asked him to picture the person in his mind, what he looked like and sounded like. What did they talk about during the sales process? (Ric always got to know a great deal about a person when he was selling a piano.)

While we were talking about everything *but* the person's

name, I also had him "find" the customer files in his cabinet, more by "feel" than by remembering where they were. Once there, we again took "another path" through Ric's brain to the information, and voila! Success! He had the folder in his hand!

I could see that lots of information was still in Ric's brain; he just needed to find a different path to access it. The path he'd been using before he'd died was "lost" during his death, so we had to make new paths around the damaged areas to find information.

This also brings to mind the experience in the hospital when Ric could make a fist with his hands when it had been too painful to do so prior to his death. I now know that pain is a pathway in the brain that can also be "erased" or, at least, "circumvented."

I still had a nagging feeling that I was missing something spiritually. I was pretty down on the God thing and the death thing, but people kept asking and I kept saying no God, no lights, no pearly gate, no nothing.

One of my favorite lines at this time was "When you die, you die; there's nothing after, but until then, there's always ice cream." I heard it on some television show and adapted it. I guess it's funny, but it did shut people up, so that was good.

Bev seemed to think that I had changed a lot, but I couldn't see it. I knew that I wasn't happy at all with my lot in life, and I didn't want to deal anymore with anything that bugged me.

Still, I wanted everyone to know, at this point, that I was grateful to be alive and for all the things people had done for me. I know it might sound like I was whining and crying, but I just wasn't able to show my thanks at that time.

Emphasis on Ric's gratitude here! I found that his love and gratitude for being here and having the "second chance" to be here to support Chiara in successfully completing high school was palpable. His apparent gratitude made up for his lack of patience, and he kept most of the "complaining" to himself.

I know that his not talking about some of the things that were going on with him contributed to his unhappiness, and what I could see was potential depression, something that Ric would never have considered allowing himself to slip into prior to his death experience.

He'd used food and television as coping mechanisms in

the more recent past, drugs and sex in the more distant past, but he'd been too self-centered and self-absorbed to allow anger, fear, and anxiety to get the best of him by way of depression.

After death, however, with the exception of television, none of those other diversions were readily available to him. Instead, Chiara and her tennis, Marshall and the music, and the San Francisco Giants and baseball were his saving graces.

At six months, things were freeing up. I'd gotten my driver's license back and was now able to take Chiara to tennis stuff and gigs. I felt like a bird flying out of the nest for the first time. In October 2010, the Giants won the World Series, and I was heading into my first holiday season.

This might have been the best holiday time in a while because the previous couple of years hadn't been easy. In 2009, I closed my business, and this caused a lot of stress for all of us.

Thank Hu for Bev, who kept working her butt off to keep us afloat. We were paycheck-to-paycheck, and every spare dime went to Chiara and her tennis, as it should. We had no vacations, no nothing extra.

In the long run, it did teach us all that we did have each

other, and that was good enough.

Just before Christmas, something amazing happened. We got a check for my back payments of disability pay for the previous year, and I started getting my monthly checks. We were saved. Bev got a dividend check from a company we didn't even know was still sending them out.

Now I know money can't solve everything, but we sure needed the uplift it gave to all of our spirits. This also meant that Marshall and I could record the CD that we'd wanted before but that either of us hadn't been able to. We had a great time doing it, and I have to say, it came out great. We're proud to have been able to do this for our family and friends. Thank Hu!

If you notice the references to HU in this writing, Ric found "HU" after his death experience. When I looked it up, I found it referenced as a sound that is "a love song to God." How appropriate, considering Ric's experience, but that came afterwards because . . .

I was still missing something. I could feel it and almost

see it, but it stayed out of my reach. I'd just have to keep looking.

2011: My First Birth-day

January 22, 2011 was my first birth-day after the event. It had been a crazy year, but I was still alive and not feeling too bad. I still didn't have much energy and what I did have I used to play gigs and go with Chiara to tennis. I knew Bev thought I hadn't changed all that much, but, believe me, I had.

I still had the smoking problem that I was hiding from everyone. I kept getting caught and lying through my teeth to cover myself. As JoAn says, addicts will do anything it takes, no matter who it hurts, including themselves.

And it did hurt. The stress was so bad, it finally put me back in the hospital because I couldn't breathe, and the fluid in my chest was so bad that I had to take shots of Lasix and pee for three hours straight. When they finally let me go, I did feel much better, but I still had my problem.

I either needed to quit smoking or tell the family to leave me alone.

Just a few paragraphs (months) previously, Ric wrote about how I thought he'd changed, but that he hadn't. Now, in the paragraph above, he wrote about how I thought he hadn't changed, but that he had.

As confusing as this sounds, I laugh now as I write about this because, as paradoxical as all this might seem, that's the Truth (with a capital T) of how our lives were.

One moment Ric, me, everything might seem that nothing had changed from the way we were before the death experience. The very next moment, it was clear that everything had changed. Sanity became a relative term, and if there had been a "normal" for the Adamo family prior to the death experience, afterwards there was never a consistency in what was needed to care for Ric and each other.

As I saw it, being able to be flexible and adaptable and to hold no expectations around literally anything was key to surviving.

The next few months were mostly the same, music and tennis, but I was getting restless. By April, my friend Marshal was getting to the point where he couldn't travel to play gigs. His cancer was knocking him down a lot, so we just did the gigs in his area.

When an opportunity came up for me to attend spring

training for the Giants in Scottsdale, I jumped on it, and the family let me go.

This would be my first big trip by myself. I was pretty scared and so were they. At least my Cousin Lynn, her husband, Bob, and my Uncle John and Aunt Jean were there, so it was great. Three games in three days. Way too cool.

Thank God again for the San Francisco Giants! What a miracle for Ric to be able to go, for the first time in his life, to spring training. His physical and mental/emotional health were still precarious, yet when he decided he wanted to make this trip to spring training, I didn't hesitate in supporting him.

I knew it would take a lot out of him, yet even if he exhausted himself literally to death, he would have died for the final time doing something that he loved. I just had to get over any anxiety I might have and let him go on the trip.

Since that was a successful trip, I got to go to Florida with Chiara to the Extreme Tennis Academy for four days of hard tennis conditioning—for her, not me—ha-

ha. We had a great time and visited some friends, Tony and Bobbie. I love having friends all over the United States from my days of travel and piano sales.

These two trips, although exhausting, were the best I'd felt so far, and they gave me hope for the future that I could have the confidence to do a lot more.

It was still there, something that I was missing. Sometimes, I thought I got it, but then it would be gone. Maybe not looking is the answer.

I'd like to take a minute to say something about heart disease. It's a strange thing to go through. I seem to feel okay. Most of the time, it takes longer to recover from doing many normal things, yet I can do them. I seemed to be tired most of the time. I wasn't sure if it was the heart or depression. I knew my heart was tired and worn out, so some of it was expected.

The depression was another story; it seemed too difficult to get over the fact that a person could drop dead any time at all. I know all of us have that same possibility, but it was different since I'd been there and knew it really could happen. It kinda wrecked any notion of invulnerability that I might have. So, I carry this knowledge around in the depths of my mind, and it can come up at any time to bite me. Talk about stress!

Stress with a capital S! For me, by this time, I was beginning to find my way out of exhaustion and into my passion for life. The intimate knowledge that I had of life *and* death were beginning to transform me and my relationships—my relationship with my Source/God, myself, my miracle husband, my daughter, my mother, etc. Wow!

Was it possible that Ric's death experience could transform those close to him as well as himself? Could I be moved more into my life by an experience that took my husband out of his life?

Spring had been fun, then arrived summer. The Giants were playing every day and so was Chiara. It was a great time; however, my friend Marshall was getting worse. We were still able to play the gigs around Lincoln where he lived. He'd quit his other band, Lincoln Highway, and was just doing solo gigs at senior centers, and four times a month he had gigs at Crossroads. I was keeping busy, and that was a good thing.

Right around that time, I had the feeling I needed to go to the mountains. It always had been the best medicine for me to hear water running down a creek and be surrounded by trees and critters of all types.

Just the fresh air and the sweetness of fresh mountain water is so healing in itself. I just had to go, and by the way, I love to fish. I just had to convince the family.

Chiara was the hardest; she couldn't get over the fact that I'd be alone in the forest. "What if you die, and I'm not there, Daddy?" This question of hers had much more meaning than it might seem. Remember Bev's idea of what happened when I died and how Chiara was somehow "tied" to me and gave me a "rope" to follow back home?

Okay, so I finally got Chiara to understand that it would be fine for me to die in the woods; nothing would make me happier. I went fishing at the same spot I had been going to for years. There I was, physically standing on the same rock from my wakeup call when I was dead. Talk about a high-powered and raw déjà vu!

At this point, it was the spring of 2011, and Ric was getting closer to the events that would help him remember what had happened while he was clinically dead. He was also on his own without me prompting him, and he was beginning to become current with his own life.

That meant that he "remembered" that his dad had passed away; he remembered the estrangement from his son;

and he remembered some of the stories that he'd told me when he'd first returned, such as his standing on the rock at the stream, talking to his dad.

It wasn't the best time to be fishing. It was raining hard, but being the tough old mountain man that I am, I went out anyway. After all, the fish don't care if it rains. I put on my rain slicker, and that was that. I was no longer able to go to some of my favorite spots; the terrain was much too tough. I did have three or four spots that I could get to, and it was a great time.

There was no one around, and over the next two days I caught a dozen trout and took in the fresh air and water. To the right, it may not have been the best thing I could have done for my body. To the left, I do believe it was the best thing I could have done for my spirit.

I think this brought me closer to where I was going.

Some of you may have noticed Ric writing about something "to the left" or "to the right." That was his expression that he used in place of "on the one hand" and "on the other hand," although I have to say that I don't remember him ever using those expressions prior to his death experience.

Maybe it's a good time for me to bring "John" into the picture, too. One of the experiences with Ric that freaked me out more than just a little was that when he first came home, "John" appeared.

Ric mentioned that he was in a lot of pain from all the chest compressions. Once some of his other issues started fading, he realized just how much pain his chest and even breathing were causing him. He couldn't walk up the stairs to our bedroom because it was too much strain on his heart, and he couldn't lie down on the bed we had downstairs; he couldn't breathe in a prone position.

We considered getting a hospital bed for him, but he suggested, "Let me try sleeping in my recliner first." We had a couch that had built-in recliners on both ends, and I have to admit that I was so afraid he would stop breathing at any moment that I didn't want to be out of the room when he was sleeping.

He slept on one end of the couch, and I slept in the recliner at the other end. It worked great, and I could still reach over and touch him to make sure he was still breathing.

Within the first week of this, as we were relaxing and I was praying that he would be able to get some rest, Ric turned his head, looked at me, and asked, "Where am I?"

After I told him we were at home, he responded, "I don't

live here." He began looking around, and from the look on his face, I could tell that he really meant it.

For whatever reason, I asked him, "Who are you?"

He answered, "John."

Oh, holy crap!

Once I learned of Ric's perspective of not knowing where he was and who people were sometimes, I realized that sometimes that even included Ric not knowing who he was! Ric didn't remember ever being "John," although after a time, I did talk to him about "John."

From that point on, it became a bit of a humorous way of his teasing me about being John instead of Ric, especially if he had done or said something about which I might take offense. I thank God for "John" because he often had us laughing instead of fighting, although I was noticing that we didn't fight anymore.

When Ric came back after dying, all of us began treating each other differently. Although Ric was so quick to temper, we all knew that this didn't change the love that we could feel for each other.

The depression that was Ric turning his fear inward and the rage that was Ric turning his fear outward were forgiven quickly and without any aftereffect.

I also found myself choosing the path of love instead of needing to be "right" about literally anything. It became more important to love and support Ric, Chiara, and my mom than anything else. Period.

When I got back home from my time fishing, summer was about to begin. This meant a lot of tennis with Chiara, and that was a good thing. She played almost every day. I got to listen to the Giants and watch her play. Really cool.

To the right! Marshal was getting worse, and all he could do any longer was play once a week at Kim's for prime rib night on Fridays. I helped him set up and tear down, so he could play. I couldn't make it every week, but I did the best I could to help out.

My other best friend Howard was getting worse also. MLS was taking its toll; he was in and out of the hospital every few days. He had stopped responding to e-mails and couldn't talk on the phone. There I was, waiting for my two best friends to die.

Other than when my dad had passed, I don't believe I'd ever felt so depressed. Most nights, I didn't sleep more than a couple of hours, unless I had really worn myself out, like at a tennis match. I just couldn't stop thinking about my friends and how I wished to spend what was left of my own life. I needed to figure it out if I was ever going to be happy again.

In August, Chiara got her driver's license. This wasn't good for my stress level, but it had to be done. I needed to let her go, and I knew I could do it, but, wow was it hard.

Baseball was still going on, and Chiara was starting high school tennis, so I was staying busy. My life with the family was hard; I just couldn't get over the fact that there was somewhere else I needed to be or something else I needed to be doing. Physically? Mentally? Emotionally? What was it?? Why couldn't I get it??

2012: My Second Birth-day

The holidays came and went, then it was time for my second birth-day, January 22, 2012. I was two years old, so I told everyone to watch out, "Here comes the terrible twos!"

I was ready to start doing some things that I'd been wanting to do for a long time; however, just about the time I'd gotten over being depressed about Marshal dying in 2011, Howard passed, then it started all over again. Sometimes a guy just can't catch a break. I went down to LA for the funeral, and while it helped, it seemed I just wasn't able to get over my loss.

While in LA, I saw my brother Michael. We had dinner and a great conversation long into the night, and it was good. I then had a six-hour drive home to reflect on life, the universe, and everything.

At this point, I was getting increasingly depressed. I couldn't play my guitar, and I didn't want to do anything except sleep, read sci-fi books, and forget about everything. My health seemed stable, but because I wasn't very active, I was getting weaker.

I needed to get back to yoga and some kind of movement. I didn't see how I could last much longer like this.

God had sent some old friends back into my life. I think this was good, but my paranoia made me think that maybe they were there to bring me down.

To the left, maybe they were there because I'd been letting go of a lot of things that had hurt me in the past, so I was open to seeing certain people again, and they were open to seeing me. Sometimes choice sucks.

Eventually I started playing my guitar again, mostly because my old high school bud and longtime bass player, Wayne, came to California for a stay before going to Florida with his son and grandkids. We were able to get ahold of other friends and play music.

It seemed music was once again my savior. When I play, all is right with the world.

I wasn't sure how my family was able to deal with me. I knew it had been hard. Sometimes, I was good; other times, I lost it.

It made me sad, and I wanted to get away so I wouldn't hurt anyone, but where could I go? It's not like I felt trapped all the time, and I would hate to not be around my daughter and wife.

The last few months had been much like the past, going to tennis and listening to the Giants. I did get to the mountains in the spring to do some fishing. It was nice, but I got sick and ended up in the hospital for three days.

It was pretty scary that just a little activity could knock me out of the game, but at least I got to watch the Giants on TV.

At this point, it had been two and a half years since I'd died. Would I ever find the answer? Hell, I would settle for even knowing the *question*!

Chapter 11

So What *Really* Happened?

I know you probably think I wasn't a very nice woman when I was screaming at God to "Take him back! Take him back!" when I was sitting in the car in the hospital parking lot, so tired I could hardly see straight and the hospital having given Ric morphine that absolutely made him crazy.

There was another time after his death experience that I felt like killing Ric. So let me tell you about that.

I've always considered myself a spiritual person, although there were times in my life when I walked away from God, mostly because I thought God had walked away from me. Those were times in my growing up when my parents were deeply embedded in their disease of alcoholism, and it seemed as though God had given me way too much to handle and that God wasn't helping me in any way, shape, or form.

Of course, looking back on those times, I know that wasn't true. At some point in my life, I realized the footprints in the sand concept, of God having been right beside me and supporting me the whole time.

In any case, at the point in my life when Ric died, I knew that God absolutely exists. I had what I considered an amazing relationship with God, with the Universe, with the Powers that Be. I felt "connected" spiritually and at peace about a lot of things that had happened during the course of my lifetime.

I have a great and unfailing faith. I know that everything happens for a reason that serves me and the highest good of all.

I also had some exposure to others who'd had "near-death experiences." When I talk about Ric, I refer to his experience as a "death experience" because he was clinically dead for 44 minutes, and even once his heart was restarted, he wasn't breathing on his own, and his essence didn't return to his body for two days.

My mom, on the other hand (to the left), at one point in her life when she was still in her alcoholism, had a grand mal seizure that resulted in her being transported in an ambulance to the hospital. During that transport, she literally died; they "lost her."

I remember my mom talking about it afterwards and that she'd thought it was so amusing because she realized that she wasn't in her physical body. She was above her body and the EMTs, observing it all. The fact that she wasn't in her body anymore didn't bother her at all. It wasn't a big deal to her that she was dead or disembodied.

Rather, she thought it was amusing that the EMTs were so bothered by the fact that their patient just died. The EMTs were able to revive her rather quickly.

When my mom talked about her near-death experience (and she could remember it vividly), she talked about it as being in this beautiful space even though she could see what was going on here on this earth. She felt completely at peace and not concerned about the circumstances.

I was familiar with this story from my mom, and, of course, I had read about other people's near-death experiences because I (like many people) was dying to find out what happens when we die.

I believe beyond any doubt that after death there's an existence that's greater and more expanded, I would even say infinite, beyond this life as a human on this planet. When Ric died and came back, there was a part of me that was really excited to learn what had happened and where he'd gone.

Some of those questions were answered in the conversations that I had with Ric after he re-entered his body at the hospital. During that first couple of days returning from the coma, Ric talked about being with his dad fishing at the stream, then playing baseball and rock and roll. I could see him doing these things as he was telling me about them.

While he was sharing his experiences of what had

happened while he was clinically dead, I could intuitively "see" him doing those things, but I wasn't quite sure if this was part of the "life flashing before your eyes" phenomenon I'd read about (called the "life review").

For his part, during those first few days after his death experience, Ric didn't "remember" telling me what he'd experienced.

After a time, when a lot of things were going better for Ric and his short-term memory loss seemed to be getting better (he could actually read pages in a book and not have to go back and re-read them the next time he picked up the book), I was looking forward to talking to him.

I didn't want to bug him about it until he was in a more stable place because I could tell that there was a lot of times that he wasn't sure what was going on. He was still getting used to being back in his body, so I was patient, and I waited and waited, until finally I asked him.

"Okay, what happened? Tell me where you were and what it was like! Tell me everything, and I can't wait to hear what you have to say!"

Ric, in his amazingly calm and debonair manner, looked at me and replied, "Well, I don't know! I was dead!"

As the silence stretched out, I literally wanted to kill him.

"What do you mean, *you don't know*? What do you mean, *you can't tell me*? You're kidding me, right?"

I then proceeded to tell him about the stories he'd told

me during the couple of days after he'd "woken up."

I could see from his eyes that those experiences weren't something that he "remembered" at all. It was as though Ric had come back with those experiences during his death, had told them to me, then promptly had forgotten them.

I wondered at the time if I had made all that up. Surely not.

I can still hear every one of Ric's words as he told me about the experience on the stream with his dad and the other reminiscences. They were real!

After that, when I would hear other people ask him what had happened, the same kind of questions I had, he would reply exactly the same, "I don't know. I was dead."

What happened? No doors, lights, mists, no floating above my body, just nothing. Even still, I don't know if it was a dream or a vision, but just before I woke up in the hospital, I found myself standing at Hat Creek, trout fishing.

This was a place where I've been many times. I knew the rock I was standing on by its first name. I looked upstream, and there was my father, standing in a certain spot, fishing where I'd seen him many times.

He had passed away a few years previously, so you can imagine my surprise.

My dad looked at me and asked, "What are you doing here? You're not supposed to be here yet. Go on back right now."

I didn't realize until later that I had other experiences too (which I'm going to share below). At the time, the next thing I had any knowledge of was seeing a nurse holding my hand, and in turn, I was thinking she must have been an angel.

Since dying, I've been having a lot of trouble with time and catching up with the timeline. It's like my mind is in warp speed about things I need to say, but I can't until I catch up to present day, so I'm just gonna start writing stuff down and try my best.

The first thing I need to say is that when I was dead, I spoke to God. How I realized this experience happened is part of a backstory, but since the conversation (now that I can remember it!) won't quit bugging me, I have to talk about it now.

This comes under the heading of *Holy Crap*! As I've said before, I didn't believe it was possible, but I guess I was wrong.

Now, I believe beyond any doubt that I did speak to God, or I should say, He spoke to me, and He really did have something to say to me.

Here we go. I'm going to get into some of it now because if I don't, I won't be able to sleep. He seems to be relentless in His desire to get some message out, and I have to be the one to tell it.

As far as I can tell, we only spoke for a minute, but then again, it felt like it was hundreds of years. (I feel like I'm full to the top with info, but I can only get it out at the right time. I don't think God cares about time at all, if there is such a thing.)

The Word of God!

"Are you kidding me? What do you people think you're doing?"

I know, I know, you'd think God would sound like some kind of profit (I can't even spell it right—profit, prophet, whatever), but that's not who I am, and God is going to talk to me in a way I can understand.

So then He says:

"Nothing much has changed in all these thousands of years. There are still starving children, people killing each other, masters and slaves, kings and politicians, greedy bankers, and out-and-out crazy people who think they know me and my will. Are you kidding me?"

He then reveals:

"Ric, here's a message for you."

[Holy Crap, here it comes].

"You cannot live without air; you have to stop smoking if you're going to help me get done what needs to be done.

"This message carries over to the rest of the world as well. I've had people go days, weeks, months, and years without food and water to make a point, but no one can survive without *air* and the stuff it's made of. Without *air*, you die. End of story. Got it? I hope so.

"Of course, it's your choice. Earth is a place that can take care of itself. I made it that way. Earthquakes, volcanoes, global warming and cooling, forest fires, all these things are part of the earth taking care of itself. You people don't have to do anything except breathe; make sure the *air* is clean and love each other."

I love this guy. He gets you, then He gets you again. So now you wonder how I know it was God speaking to me. Well, here it is: I'm so far away from being green or any kind of environmentalist, and He used my smoking as a metaphor for the whole world. Where else could I possibly have gotten the idea if it wasn't from God?

Now, He hasn't given me specific instruction on what He wants me to do, and my daughter is afraid He'll tell me to blow something up or hurt somebody, but she watches too many scary movies. Those kinds of things are not in my playbook. The only thing I know for sure is that I think I better figure out how to quit smoking, then we shall see.

Wow, so Ric actually *was* talking with God! Oh wait! Excuse me! Ric made the clarification that it was God who was talking to him. Ric, in fact, was pretty much dumbstruck by the fact when he realized that God *was* talking to *him*!

I can absolutely guarantee that this was God talking to Ric because nobody *but* God could have told Ric that he had to stop smoking, then Ric actually took that to heart and was willing to try to quit!

When Ric first told me about all this, two years after he came back from death, I was dumbfounded for so many reasons, not the least of which was that Ric was going to do something that I didn't think would happen in any of his lifetimes—Ric was willing to figure out how to stop smoking!

That's the true miracle and spiritual healing that I began to recognize more and more with Ric. The impossible was in that moment truly possible.

I started asking myself, "If God were talking to *me*, what would he say?" I slapped myself (softly) on the forehead and reminded myself that God had been talking to me all my life, and I was, at that point in my life, pretty good at listening and paying attention and actually taking inspired action based (mostly) on what God told me to do.

Now my question is, what do I think is impossible, but if God told me to do it, would actually be possible?

I'm asking God to help me write these next words because, as a human being, I'm not sure I can adequately convey the love, respect, honor, and awe that I have for Ric Adamo. My husband. Chiara's father. What extraordinary strength, courage, and downright grit he has shown throughout our marriage and most particularly in these experiences we're sharing with you now in this book.

I would love to be able to tell you that Ric has quit smoking and is the most agreeable and perfect partner/husband in the world, yet, even while those two things are not true and our lives are still a bit "messy," I wouldn't trade places with anyone.

I love and live with a bona-fide miracle. Of course, that was always true, but it simply took his death for it to become crystal clear to me. The "messiness" of life, the struggles are what make the celebrations and the successes so much more meaningful.

Ric and I are both now open to anything and everything, so watch out world—here we come!

My challenge to you, Divine Reader, is in this question—what about you? Does God (you choose your own word/description that works) talk to you? And if She/He/It does, do you listen and act? What would be the one message that you *know* that *God* would say to you? What are YOUR Three Reasons for being here?

What do you think is impossible but if Spirit told you or even asked you to do it, would then become possible? What are you waiting for?

You, Divine Reader, are meant to accomplish awesome endeavors and live your unique life. All the seeds for making your dreams come true are within you. There is nothing you lack or need to wait for.

You have now been invited to stop "dying your death" and start truly living your life! Ric was "dying his death" until January 20, 2010. Through his 44 minutes of death, he brought back with him Three Reasons that made all of his past and current struggles worth every minute of life that he can live now.

Find *your* Three Reasons and *go for it*! I promise you that your life, even through any challenges, will take on a consistent and fantastic message of fun, magic, and miracles! If Ric could die and return against all odds, you, right now from where you are, can *do this*!

Chapter 12

My Three Reasons – *Your* Three Reasons

I've been a writer all of my life, even before I learned how to write. By that, I mean that I was always imagining stories and telling them to others (fiction writer) and understanding how things worked and could work (self-help/inspirational nonfiction writer).

In the early 1980s, when I first started moving out of my "dark journey of the soul" and into the light, I wrote *Arguments with God,* as a counterpoint to Neale Donald Walsh's magnificent *Conversations with God* series.

At that point in my life, I was discovering my tremendous connection with Source. I was receiving all kinds of intuitive messages and Divine guidance, and I was just as likely to argue with all of it rather than follow it.

Over the years, of course, I did learn that Divine guidance was so much better to follow than what I could come up with on my own. Being in a state of observation with respect to everything that happened during Ric's death experience and journey back into life enabled me to access some deep Divine energy that kept me going.

During the course of everything that happened with Ric, I was still working my full-time job, which meant that, sometimes, I was starting my workday as early as 4 or 5 in the morning to be home in time to take Ric to his many doctor appointments.

He had a lot of them, neurology, psychology, speech therapy (having to do with the fact that he was intubated, although there was absolutely nothing wrong with Ric's speech per se, etc.) He was glib, and I had to work doubly hard because Ric could convince medical personnel that he was doing much better than he really was.

At certain points, some doctors and nurses were on the brink of being convinced that I was the one who needed the care, not Ric! Jeez!

In any case, I was also working to keep the household together and provide Chiara with attention she needed and help her to move through all the emotional turmoil that you can imagine was going on with her.

Thank goodness for her innate intelligence and fantastic resilience—and her loving her dad and me, no matter what!

Thank goodness also for my mom. She was amazing in helping support all of us in the daily life of making sure we had food, clean clothes, and a clean house. My mom was a mainstay of our home during this time.

Still, I was the person on whom the main pressure to make this all work lay. I could feel that pressure directly on my shoulders. Even with all the awesome support from medical personnel and my immediate family, I had, by necessity, pretty much shut myself down from anything except taking care of my family—financially, mentally, emotionally, and spiritually—without asking for help.

After a full year of all this caretaking, I was spent. At that time, I asked God to tell me what to do, and I promised that I wouldn't argue.

Interestingly enough, I was told by my higher guidance to go to a one-day workshop in a city about sixty miles from where I lived, so I went.

The workshop was on January 20, 2011, exactly one year from the date Ric had died. The journey there was challenging in that I got lost; the address in the email about the event was incorrect. That was before I had a smart phone, etc. I literally pulled off the freeway and stopped my car on a side street and started to cry.

It was one of those crossroads that I normally would not have identified until later in hindsight, yet I knew, in that moment, that I was being given a choice. I could either find a way to get to the workshop, or I could give up and go home.

I took a deep breath and decided I was going to find a way to get to the workshop. I was able to contact Chiara by phone and ask her to go into my email and get me the phone number of the hotel. When I called them and learned that I was in the wrong city, they gave me directions.

I found my way to the hotel, parked my car, walked into the hotel, and met an Earth Angel called Maggie.

I had originally met Maggie years before and, at that time, had only spent a few minutes talking with her. There was something about this meeting years later that embarked both of us on a challenging and most rewarding journey of friendship and business partnership.

My friendship with Maggie led me to other friends and teachers, including May 25, 2011, when I met Sandy.

Sandy is an intuitive coach, and after having known her for only a short time, I began calling her the "super Google of the spiritual realm." Sandy helped me so much over the course of the next two years not only in bringing my own life into clearer focus, but also in helping Ric see and understand what had happened to him.

I remember telling Sandy my frustration with Ric. "What do you mean, you don't remember anything about what happened?" I told Sandy that if he hadn't just died, I probably would have killed him! I've always been a metaphysical enthusiast because of many experiences of my own over the years (that would be a whole 'nother book), and it was quite excruciating to know that I was living with a man who literally had a conversation with God, returned, and couldn't talk about it because he "didn't remember anything."

At no time did Sandy "tell" Ric what had happened to him. The best way I can describe what happened is that Sandy asked questions and allowed Ric to experience the "reliving" of his journey in a safe and non-threatening space.

Thanksgiving of 2012 was when Ric had the epiphany that he had, in fact, talked with God, or rather, that God had talked to him. It was as miraculous as when Ric came back into his body.

Bev's Three Reasons

In August 2013, Ric and I were invited to speak on a radio show about our experiences of life, death, and life. During the interview, the host asked me a question I wasn't expecting: "Bev, what are *your* Three Reasons? Do you have Three Reasons for being here?"

Without hesitation, I answered, "Absolutely!"

What I said and what I know now is this:

The *First Reason* that I'm here is to lead others to the truth of who they are. That includes me as well! Through this journey with Ric, I came to see that I've always seen the Truth (with a capital T) about people.

I see the miraculous and Divine human being and his/her purpose for being on this planet. I've always been able to see this about others, and, as a young girl, it scared others to be seen so completely by another person, especially a little girl.

I equated their fear as telling me that there was something wrong with me, so, like many others who begin life knowing who they are and why they're here, I began hiding my gift and myself from the world (that "dark journey of the soul" about which I spoke earlier).

My *Second Reason* for being here is to create—to create in a way that's different from most of the messy ways that I learned growing up.

Instead, I'm a creator in an expansive way, through the miraculous and magical way I learned from being married to Ric and being willing to live a most amazing life.

I create out of chaos and dysfunction and from some of the darkest things that can happen to a human being. Using my earlier experiences, I transform the darkness into a lightness to create an understanding that all things serve.

My creations come in the form of books, and through speaking and teaching, I can create and lead a movement of people in which I guide them in transforming their minds, bodies, and even their businesses and daily lives, to match their magnificent Spirits.

The *Third Reason* that I'm here, the icing on the cake, is magic! My heart just sings (literally) when I think about doing magic!

While I can totally appreciate the magic of magicians

who work with illusion to create experiences that "appear" to be magic, the magic about which I speak involves working with the veil of illusion and pulling back that curtain, so I and others can experience the magic that's inherent in all of us—the magic of the moment and the connection of everything in this life.

If you ever had the opportunity to watch the first season of the television show *Touch*, you'll be able to see what I mean by real magic. Real, conscious, practical magic is something best experienced first-hand, and I can help facilitate such firsthand experiences for people.

Your Three Reasons

The aim of this chapter of the book is *you*, Divine Reader— *you* are the focus of this chapter. I'm profoundly grateful for being able to share My Three Reasons with you here, and it's time to move to the crux of this book: *Your* Three Reasons!

I've already invited you to consider what the message would be that *only* God could deliver to you and that you would be willing to hear and act upon.

This message is something that either scares the hell out of you to consider doing or something that you find yourself *totally* resistant to doing, to the point of even making you physically nauseous to even think about (remember how resistant to even considering stopping smoking Ric was!).

Now you're being invited to know what *Your* Three

Reasons are, without having to go through the tremendously difficult reboot involved with dying, talking to God wherever you would go to have that conversation, then returning with a jolting and terror-producing journey back into yourself!

Ric would absolutely tell you that what I'm inviting you to do is so much more pleasant than what he went through . . . so here goes.

Don't think about it. Don't worry about it. Don't stress about it. Relax and envision yourself on that radio show.

The host turns to you and asks, "So, Divine Reader, what are Your Three Reasons? Do you have Three Reasons for being here in this life?"

Next you answer most enthusiastically and without hesitation, "Yes! Absolutely!"

Now, state Your Three Reasons!

Profound truth is always simple. You may find that later you'll want to return to think about those reasons and allow them to expand as you consider your path to this moment and what you wish to create as you move forward in the moments of your life.

Let me add that I have all kinds of ideas and ways in which you can have fun playing with Your Three Reasons. It's who I am and what I do!

Feel free to get in touch with me, and I would love to tell you what I "see."

Get ready for your interview. Your life is ready for you!

Chapter 13

The Last Word

First—Bev's Last Word

Perhaps you're wondering why did Ric and I wait more than six years to write this most amazing story?

I didn't have writer's block. I didn't forget any part of this adventure. How could I have? This entire experience is hard-wired into my brain. I have to confess that I was afraid to write it. I was afraid to "finish the book."

You see, there was a part of me that was convinced that if I finished the book, then Ric would die again, only this time it would be for keeps, forever.

When people asked me if I was worried about Ric when he went fishing by himself in the mountains for days on end, when he travelled to Arizona for the SF Giants spring training games, or when he went to Florida with Chiara to watch her play tennis at an academy, I would always say that I wasn't worried in the least. That is and was the complete truth.

Had Ric died during one of those adventures, he would have died happy and content. How crazy was it that I thought my writing this story might kill him?

What I realized was that this book took me to the crux of *My* Three Reasons! Writing this book scared the hell out of me, and I was *totally* resistant to doing it! (Sound familiar? See previous chapter on finding Your Three Reasons!) I overcame this resistance by knowing my Reasons and living them.

The Reasons are powerful beyond measure, so if you haven't found *Your* Reasons, **Go back and do it now**! Your life will change immeasurably and miraculously.

Ric's dying and return to life is a heroic adventure of epic proportions and, over the years, as I shared bits and pieces of it with others, I came to understand that recording this experience in writing and sharing it with others could actually serve people.

I was told that people would read it and be inspired to ask themselves, "What *are* My Three Reasons for being alive? Am I dying my death by dwelling in a shroud of negativity? Can I start living my life from a perspective that everything happens for a reason, and in my life, it happens because it serves me in living from my heart and with purpose?"

Where do we go from here?

Only God knows. If I continue to be open and listen, I'll

always know what my next step is, even if that's the only step I'm shown in the moment, and I'm totally okay with that.

I have my Reasons for being here. I'm living my life to the best of my ability and having *big fun* while making a positive difference in other people's lives.

I've been given such a gift of witnessing and living a miracle with my husband Ric, and, with him as well, creating our own miracle!

Blessings, magic, and miracles to you all!

Bev Adamo

Second—A Word From Our Miracle

My name is Chiara Adamo. I was fifteen years old on January 20, 2010, when my dad died. His heart just stopped, but this isn't a story about death—it's a story about baseball and miracles.

My dad grew up in Napa, California, and of all the stories he used to tell me, and you know dads—they like to tell stories—anyway, of all the stories, the best were the stories he would tell about his dad taking him and his younger brother to baseball games at Candlestick Park in San Francisco to see the Giants play.

Dad was born in 1951, so when the Giants moved to San Francisco when he was a kid, Dad explained, "That just about made my life perfect!" He would tell me that they went to as many games as they could, and even when he grew up and was travelling around the country playing rock and roll, or later when he met my mom and "settled down," he still believed that every baseball season was going to be "the one."

The World Series title was only a season away as far as my dad was concerned, no matter what the "experts" said or what kind of record the team had.

So, back to January 20, 2010—my dad died surrounded by family and friends at a café in my hometown. They started CPR right away, but even after the EMTs arrived and gave him two or three big shocks, it was pretty clear that he was gone.

They loaded his body into the ambulance, and my mom, grandma, and I followed it to the hospital. The ambulance had its lights on, but no siren, and we weren't breaking any speeding laws getting there.

After we had been waiting in the emergency room for twenty minutes or so, the nurse came out to lead us back to where my dad's body was. When we walked in and the doctor began to talk to us, we had to ask the doctor to repeat what he'd just said because he didn't tell us that my dad was gone as we'd expected. The doctor told us that they were able to get my dad's heart restarted!

Dad couldn't breathe on his own; he was hooked up to a machine with a breathing tube down his throat, and I could hear the machine taking the breaths for him.

The doctor told us at least five times that this "never happens," that "it's not like on TV." I actually think the doctor was more surprised than we were that my dad's heart was beating again!

But dang! No heartbeat and not breathing for over forty minutes? That couldn't be good . . .

Much as we were told not to expect too much, I just got the idea in my head that my dad wasn't supposed to die that day, that he would be back.

Hmmmmph, I was right! His comeback was awesome (my mom calls it his "recovery"), and now she's written this book about everything.

I've told you a little about the miracles part, and here's what it has to do with baseball, at least the way my mom tells it.

She spent a lot of time with my dad, especially the first week after he came back to his body (after about two days in a coma). Mom said that there were three reasons that my dad came back.

First is me, of course! Okay, all of his family. Second is because he and his best friend had a CD to record of their original songs (which they did record, in case you ever want to hear it), and third, what my mom calls the "deal maker" or "the icing on the cake" is that once my dad was on his way to wherever you go when you die, he could "see" everything from the beginning of time to the end of time, and from that place, he saw that his San Francisco Giants were going to win the World Series!

That's when his heart started beating again in the emergency room, surprising the heck out of everyone in that room.

My dad is a walking miracle every day that he's alive. His heart is bad, and even though I was still technically a kid, I wasn't going to try to kid myself that he was going to be around forever, not like I'd believed before he'd died the first time.

I'm here to tell you, and the world, that just like in 2010 when I knew my dad was going to beat the odds and live, I know that it's possible for other miracles to happen.

I know that I'm a lucky kid. I learned a hard lesson in 2010, and I don't take anything for granted anymore— well, hardly anything.

I don't exactly know how to end this, except to say

thank you for listening, and I appreciate you knowing that miracles can happen!

Live without regrets and always tell people you love them!

With a loving heart, CHIARA

Last—The Last Word from the Man, Himself

Let me end by sharing the things I've learned. There is a God or universal energy that created the universe and all that dwells in it, whether it's us or someone else. Everything is connected, and we've been given the ability to manifest whatever we want in this life. It's our choice.

I believe that the only real thing that was given to us is love. It's the key to everything as shown by my daughter's love that wouldn't let me go; such power is the foundation of everything else.

Love people, love life, love the earth and all its beings and living things. War, greed, and hate are the downfall of us all. God gave us love and air to breathe. All else *we* create, so be careful what you ask for; it will happen.

I still have my issues with smoking, rage, depression, and some distrust of all around me, but I believe that I have the power to create a better life for myself, and I'm doing so.

Bev always says that I have to have the last word, and I'm smart enough to know that when I do *get* the last word, it's because she's kind enough to let me say my piece before the end.

What I want you to know is that I went a long way, to infinity, and came back to bring you the information in this book.

I always had this vision that I would have a chance to speak to a lot of people and in the process change the world in a positive way, make a difference, and maybe even make up for being such a self-centered asshole for so many years of my life.

I just want to say thanks because, if you're reading this, you *are* giving me that chance.

Love to all,

Ciao,

Ric Adamo

THE END . . . THE BEGINNING . . .

Acknowledgments

It has taken a Universe to raise this amazing "child" AKA The Three Reasons. So let's do this!

Profound gratitude to **God** for putting me on this planet at this time, to live this most unique and amazing life! **Ric** for being my unfailing support and love throughout this miraculous journey as his wife and life partner! **Chiara** for helping me to grow up along with her and discover that I am an awesome mom! My loving family, **Mom, Cliff, John** and my **Dad** (who has watched all this from above)! **Marshal** for his fantastic music! **The San Francisco Giants** for being the pivotal Reason Ric came back!

My magical friends, **Maggie, Jean Kathryn, Susan** and **Mary**! My passion quest muse **Alexa**! My kick-ass, badass Coach, **Emily**! My eloquent partner in this writing and healing process, **Tara**. My super hero colleagues **Amber, Cary** and **Melissa**! My fierce and professional Editor (with a capital E) **Mike**! My beautiful cover designer **Ida**! My fabulous formatter **Heidi**! And everyone else who along the way has supported and assisted me.......THANK YOU!!!

Last, and surprisingly not least, I acknowledge myself for being willing to share this most intimate and meaningful part of my life in the knowing that someone's life will be touched and changed by the courage it took to write and publish The Three Reasons!

About the Author

Bev Adamo has experienced the miracle of life, death and rebirth from the unique and inspiring experience of her husband Ric dying in her arms, then fighting his way back to life for Three Reasons. She has used this experience in her work as an inspiring speaker, author, and innovation catalyst, working with individuals and teams to transform their bodies, minds, and businesses to match their Spirits. Bev has a master's degree in organizational development and management, as well as having served in executive positions in both the public and private sectors.

Bev is a certified Dream Coach, a True Purpose Coach, an Ordained Minister and is the founder of the movement of humans who are ready to stop wearing their power (i.e., weight, worry, debt, guilt, and shame) and start owning and using their power to change their personal worlds and the world around them. Bev does this by supporting others in discovering the Three Reasons for themselves.

If you're interested in finding out more about, Bev Adamo *and* about *Your* Three Reasons, you are invited to contact her, so you can stop dying your death and start living your *life*!

www.creativehearts.com/thethreereasons

Made in the USA
San Bernardino, CA
02 April 2017